The Book of the
VELOCETTE

A Guide to twin- and single-cylinder
models including the Viceroy Scooter

Ferrers Leigh

ANNOUNCEMENT

By special arrangement with the original publishers of this book, Sir
Isaac Pitman & Son, Ltd., of London, England, we have secured the exclusive
publishing rights for this book, as well as all others in THE MOTORCYCLIST'S
LIBRARY.

Included in THE MOTORCYCLIST'S LIBRARY are complete instruction man-
uals covering the care and operation of respective motorcycles and engines;
valuable data on speed tuning, and thrilling accounts of motorcycle race
events. See listing of available titles elsewhere in this edition.

We consider it a privilege to be able to offer so many fine titles to our
customers.

FLOYD CLYMER
Publisher of Books Pertaining to Automobiles and Motorcycles

2125 W. PICO ST.   **LOS ANGELES 6, CALIF.**

INTRODUCTION

Welcome to the world of digital publishing ~ the book you now hold in your hand, while unchanged from the original edition, was printed using the latest state of the art digital technology. The advent of print-on-demand has forever changed the publishing process, never has information been so accessible and it is our hope that this book serves your informational needs for years to come. If this is your first exposure to digital publishing, we hope that you are pleased with the results. Many more titles of interest to the classic automobile and motorcycle enthusiast, collector and restorer are available via our website at www.VelocePress.com. We hope that you find this title as interesting as we do.

NOTE FROM THE PUBLISHER

The information presented is true and complete to the best of our knowledge. All recommendations are made without any guarantees on the part of the author or the publisher, who also disclaim all liability incurred with the use of this information.

TRADEMARKS

We recognize that some words, model names and designations, for example, mentioned herein are the property of the trademark holder. We use them for identification purposes only. This is not an official publication.

INFORMATION ON THE USE OF THIS PUBLICATION

This manual is an invaluable resource for the classic motorcycle enthusiast and a "must have" for owners interested in performing their own maintenance. However, in today's information age we are constantly subject to changes in common practice, new technology, availability of improved materials and increased awareness of chemical toxicity. As such, it is advised that the user consult with an experienced professional prior to undertaking any procedure described herein. While every care has been taken to ensure correctness of information, it is obviously not possible to guarantee complete freedom from errors or omissions or to accept liability arising from such errors or omissions. Therefore, any individual that uses the information contained within, or elects to perform or participate in do-it-yourself repairs or modifications acknowledges that there is a risk factor involved and that the publisher or its associates cannot be held responsible for personal injury or property damage resulting from the use of the information or the outcome of such procedures.

WARNING!

One final word of advice, this publication is intended to be used as a reference guide, and when in doubt the reader should consult with a qualified technician.

Preface

THE LE model Velocette appeals to many thousands of people not themselves enthusiastic motor-cyclists in the accepted sense of the term. This handbook accordingly only deals with such operations as can be carried out by a non-technical owner. No attempt has been made to cover any overhaul work recommended by Veloce Ltd. as more suitable for the dealer's service department. Where such work is involved the fact is clearly stated.

The book covers the following models—

LE Marks I, II and III, 149 c.c. and 192 c.c. twins, the Valiant and Vogue twins, the Viceroy scooter, the early Velocette singles MOV and MAC; the KSS and KTS, the Viper and Venom and Thruxton singles. Where special information is needed the owner should write to Veloce Ltd., Box 275, Hall Green Works, Birmingham 28, giving the frame and engine numbers of the model.

The author wishes to acknowledge his grateful thanks to Veloce Ltd. for their ready assistance in supplying technical information about their new models; and, similarly, to Amal Ltd. for a valuable table (*see* page 108) giving correct Amal carburettor settings for Velocette machines.

F. L.

Contents

The Twin-Cylinder Velocettes
1 The 150 and Early 200 LE Machines

Since the LE Velocette marks a definite attempt to design a "car on two wheels" for the benefit of those who would not normally take to a motor-cycle, certain features of the design should be specially examined and understood. (Owners of the 4-speed Mk. III machine should also see page 56.)

Notice first that it does not have to be raised upon its stand. Indeed when the machine is on a flat surface, with the tyres properly inflated and the cycle held vertical, both feet of the centre stand, one at each side, actually clear the ground. Allowed to rest, the LE leans to one side or the other, supported on its tyres and one foot of the stand.

Because of this no muscular effort is needed to roll it into the standing position, an important point to a woman. To put it on the stand all the rider needs to do is to press down with the toes on the projection at the rear edge of the footboard at one side or the other, thus swinging the spring-loaded stand down. At the same time the machine is wheeled slightly backwards.

This solves the problem of making the machine sufficiently weighty for it to be stable on wet or greasy roads—it scales 260 lb, over two hundredweight, but is easy to manipulate without exertion. How safe it is one finds as soon as the machine is ridden. The low-poised engine brings the centre of gravity well down and almost eliminates any tendency to skid.

Easy Wheel-changing. One discovers, as explained in detail later, that though neither wheel comes clear of the ground when the machine is on its stand, it is perfectly simple to raise either wheel, again without any display of strength. Each wheel is quickly detachable by the removal of one stout spindle bolt.

The Stand. On models up to 1952 the LE can be taken off its stand either by wheeling it forward, when the support clicks up automatically, or by means of the hand starting lever. This lever was interconnected so that its first movement raised the stand. On post-1952 models the lever and stand are not interconnected. Mk. III models of the LE have a kick-start and a normal roll-on stand.

The Engine. This, as just mentioned, is hung low in the frame. Both the early pre-1950 model "150" (149 c.c.) and the model "200" (192 c.c.) are water-cooled side-valve flat-twins. This two-cylinder design gives smoothness, good balance, and low weight distribution. Water cooling, though calling for a little attention in frosty weather, has several advantages. Mechanical sounds are quietened and this helps to earn the model its remarkable freedom from "motor-cycle" noise.

Footboards, in place of the usual rests, give comfort to the normally-dressed rider, accentuated by the legshields and deep

FIG. 1. THE LE VELOCETTE MKS. I–II
(*By courtesy of "Motor Cycling"*)

mudguarding. Each legshield is also used to carry, at the top, a small instrument panel. On the left one is the speedometer with a luminous hand and a marking of luminous paint at the "30" figure. The Mk. III machine up to 1966 has the instruments and switches in the headlamp cowl (*see* page 56).

Electrical Controls. These are mounted at the top of the right-hand legshield. Early models had two switches with a red warning light between them, the right-hand switch for the coil ignition, the left-hand one for the lights.

When the ignition switch is turned to the right the red light glows to indicate the flow of current through the coil, and goes out at running speeds. Veloce Ltd. have envisaged an emergency in which the rider might have a discharged battery, or even temporarily no battery at all. By turning the switch to the left the engine can be started, and run at low speeds, without the battery.

LE Mk. II models have, at the top of the right legshield, one switch with a central key, and to its left an ammeter. In this case there is no warning light. The removable key locks the switch at either OFF or PARK, a useful thief-proof device.

Starting the Machine. On models up to 1958 (Mks. I-II) one finds, at the near side and close by the bend in the water hose, a

FIG. 2. LIGHTING, IGNITION, STARTING, AND
GEAR CONTROLS (MKS. I–II)

A = Petrol tank cap.	E = Red warning light.
B = Tool box.	F = Ignition switch (also controls
C = Lighting switch (ammeter here	lights when ammeter fitted).
on most LE 200 models).	G = Starting handle (also retracts
D = Gear lever.	stand on models up to 1952)

petrol tap which pushes in for ON.* Also by the bend in the hose, and held to it by a rubber clip, is the eyeletted rod that controls the easy-start device in the carburettor. To operate, it is pulled out leftwards.

Now the rider stands, supporting the machine between the knees. Pulling gently up on the starting handle, the ratchet and pawl of the starting gear will be felt to mesh with each other. This movement must be made slowly and gently. Once the ratchet is felt to engage, a brisker movement in the same direction will turn the engine round. Continue to the end of the stroke, let the ratchet feel its way back to the beginning, and repeat. Give the engine two or three spins.

* *In for OFF: Mk. III.*

It will be noticed that nothing has yet been said about switching on. After an overnight stand, or some hours in cool weather, a few preliminary spins in this way will get the engine fully charged with mixture. As will be seen in the chapter on the carburettor the machine has a long induction pipe, and this like everything else gets cold. Obviously the engine cannot fire until there is a proper

Fig. 3. Nearside View of Engine

A = Clutch adjuster.
B = Carburettor pilot screw.
C = Petrol tap.
D = Carburettor start control.
E = Petrol filter.
F = Induction pipe.
G = Oil filler cap (engine).
H = Ignition/generator unit.
J = Dipstick (engine).

K = Oil filler (gearbox).
L = Gearbox drain plug.
M = Cylinder drain plug.
N = Cylinder head nut.
O = Footbrake.
P = Silencer.
Q = Prop stand (nearside leg).
R = Exhaust pipe (nearside).

mixture actually in the cylinders. Two or three pulls should ensure this at all times. Later models have the induction pipe protected against condensation.

To switch on one must release the starting handle and must remember to re-engage the ratchet gently as the handle is once more pulled up. If all is in order the engine will fire at once. The easy-start device automatically increases the engine speed so there is no need to twist at the throttle.

Alternatively the engine may be walk-started. Stand beside the cycle, pull out the easy-start control (and of course open the petrol tap) and put the gear lever into second gear (easier for a walk-start than first). Switch on the ignition, pull up the clutch lever, walk two or three steps with the machine and while walking release the clutch lever. The engine will quickly fire, when of course the clutch lever should be whipped out again and the gear lever returned to neutral.

The three gears on the LE are controlled by a lever with a "gate" of car type, but of opposite movement to the standard car gear-change. The 4-speed Mk. III model has a foot change gear control of normal motor-cycle type (*see* page 56).

Finding the Gears. A simple drill can be followed to avoid any temptation to look down at the lever. Press the hand inwards with the knee, at the same time moving the lever downwards, to engage first. This will prevent getting into top by mistake. Second is found by an upwards and outwards movement through neutral of course. (This is quite easy because there is only one fully upwards movement.) Top follows when the hand is turned slightly sideways, pressing the lever outwards at the same time that it is pushed straight down. The outward pressure prevents any chance of wandering back into first speed.

It is worth noting that the hand starter can be used with the clutch held out and, say, first gear engaged. This is useful if one stalls the engine on a hill. On early LEs the starting mechanism is behind the clutch, whereas the kick-start as on the LE Mk. III drives the engine through the clutch.

Few Controls. The LE is completely free from hand controls for spark, air and so on. There is only the easy-start device, which can be pushed in as soon as the engine has run for a few seconds. The spark on early machines was fixed, and the rider must change down fairly soon to stop pinking, and must use the indirect gears at low speeds or snatch and "judder" may occur in the drive. This slight loss of flexibility is the only drawback about a fixed spark.

Most machines later than mid-1950s had automatically varied ignition timing. They also had the more flexible 200 engine with its general performance greatly improved, particularly with a pillion passenger.

Thus all the rider of any model has to do when on the road is to operate the clutch lever (left-hand control), the twist-grip throttle (right hand; turn inwards to open), and the gear lever. The perfectionist, desiring to match the silence of the machine with smooth and inaudible gear changes, will realize that it takes a little time to move the right hand between gear lever and twist-grip. Thus the throttle should not be completely closed when making upward changes if a perfectly smooth accession of speed is to be obtained, and it should of course be left quite appreciably open when changing down.

Making Smooth Changes. There are no tricks about the gears. First to second is a quick change, best made straight through with no pause in neutral. Second to top requires a slight pause, and it is sometimes an advantage to let the clutch in as the gear is engaged rather than after it has gone home.

Change down, as just advised, on a fairly open throttle. The gear lever is then pulled straight up from top to second, or straight

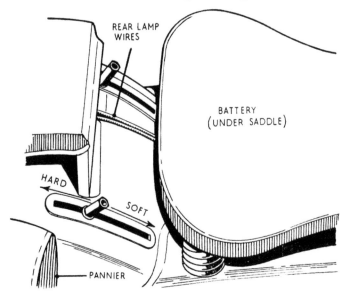

FIG. 4. REAR SUSPENSION ADJUSTMENT AND
BATTERY POSITION

On dualseat models the entire seat is hinged for lifting.

down from second to first as the case may be, as quickly as possible. Practice will determine the exact moments at which to release and engage the clutch, and how to perform double-declutching. Naturally, with the four-speed model, the gear change gives all the advantages of the foot-change system.

A Clean Design. Returning to the model, cleanness is emphasized by the complete absence of exposed moving parts, and in particular of chains. Final drive is by shaft and bevel, the shaft enclosed in a stationary, jointed torque tube. This resists the tendency to twist the engine round instead of the rear wheel.

Great comfort is given by the rear suspension. Immediately behind the saddle are two long slots in the rear mudguard, with a long nut projecting above each. When the nuts are slackened,

moved right forward, and retightened, the suspension gives
maximum softness. At the other end the adjustment provides
full firmness. The long nuts, which should always be level with
each other, are normally placed at the halfway position.

To get the best from the suspension keep the tyres at 20 lb
front and 28 lb rear for a solo rider up to 12 stone. When a pillion

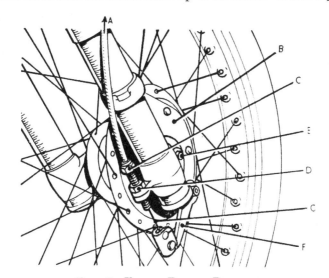

FIG. 5. FRONT BRAKE DETAILS

A = Connexion to handlebar lever. E = End of hub spindle.
B = Torque plate. F = Brake lever.
C = Adjuster. G = Cable.
D = Lock-nut.
(*Compare with Fig.* 19, *page* 50)

passenger is carried, the rear tyre must be inflated to 32 lb.
(Equivalent kilogramme figures are: 1·4, 2·0, 2·3.)

Brake Operation. Brakes on the LE follow sound conventional
practice. The right handlebar lever works an internal expanding
front hub brake and the pedal at the left footboard, emerging
from beneath the near-side cylinder head, actuates a similar brake
in the rear wheel. The four brake shoes, two in each wheel, are
identical, and are adjusted by simple screwed sleeves. Details of
operation and maintenance are given on a later page.

The wise rider will cultivate the habit of applying both brakes
together, with, if anything, slightly more application on the front
wheel. Under braking the downward pressure of the front tyre
on the road is markedly increased in the LE model.

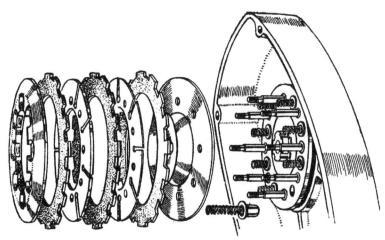

FIG. 6. POSITIONS OF THE VARIOUS MEMBERS OF THE
CLUTCH ASSEMBLY

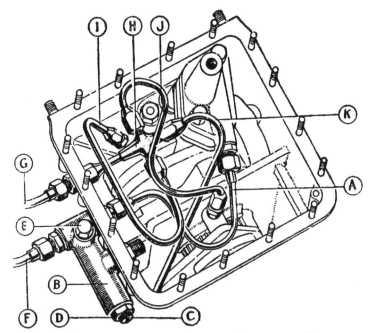

FIG. 7. ENGINE: INTERNAL OIL PIPES SEEN FROM UNDERSIDE

A = Oil pipe—pump to pressure
    release valve.
B = Oil pressure release-valve body.
C = Oil pressure adjusting screw.
D = Oil pressure adjuster lock-nut.
E = Oil pressure valve-body bolt.

F = Oil pipe—to filter.
G = Oil pipe—from filter.
H = Oil distributor-block assembly.
I = Oil pipe—to flywheel shaft bearings.
J = Oil pipe—to crankcase bearing.
K = Oil pipe—to reduction gear plate.

Road Performance. The 150 model, which ceased in 1950, gives, when in good condition, an average mileage per gallon of petrol of 100. Although the ignition is fixed, no great disadvantage results from the use of commercial-grade fuel, save that a rider in hilly country may find the machine pinking; and premium grades of fuel reduce this. Maximum speed is 40–45 m.p.h.

A maximum speed 5–10 m.p.h. higher, and a petrol consumption of about 95 m.p.g., can be expected from the LE 200, the model in latest production. A pillion passenger can be carried without difficulty over even the steepest hills.

Construction and Maintenance. Engine, gearbox, and final drive are intended to run for long periods without major attention. They are carried in a sub-frame, the backbone of the machine being a girder-like structure.

With the Mark II the machine can be separated in twenty minutes by what amounts to the withdrawal of the engine-rear wheel unit from the frame; the front wheel-frame assembly is in fact lifted away. The operation can be performed by one man, apart from the actual lifting off, and full details are given by Veloce Ltd.

Several individual operations can be performed easily enough by the owner who takes a pride in the good running of the machine. These are described in the pages that follow and are carried out with ordinary tools.

Lubrication*. *Engine sump* ($1\frac{3}{4}$ pt—2·1 U.S.—1 litre): change oil every 1,200 miles (1,920 km), using S.A.E. 30.

Fabric oil-filter, renew each 10,000 miles (16,000 km).

Gearbox and final drive ($\frac{1}{4}$ pt each—0·3 U.S.—142 c.c.): Change both every 3,000 miles (4,800 km), using S.A.E. 50.

Front forks ($\frac{1}{8}$ pt each—0·15 U.S.—72 c.c.): S.A.E. 30. Check occasionally that there is no leakage visible. Maintenance is unnecessary unless forks are dismantled (special tools needed). Refill by removing screwed caps at fork tops.

* Winter and summer, use the same grades.

2 Decarbonizing the LE

BRISK performance from a small engine is a feature common to both the 149 c.c. and 192 c.c. LE Velocettes. The clever and unusual combustion chamber design which brings this about can be appreciated as soon as one or other of the cylinder heads is

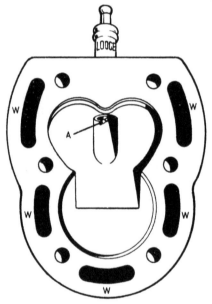

FIG. 8. CYLINDER HEAD SHOWING COMBUSTION CHAMBER

A = Plug firing points. *W* = Water jacket.

removed. Carbon formation should therefore not be allowed to develop beyond the point at which performance is impaired.

The cylinder heads contain steeply sloping pockets into which the valves rise, giving high turbulence. The combustion area above the piston is also unusual. In the majority of conventional engines this forms a recess above the piston crown, but in the LE design the opposite effect is found. That part of the head casting which comes over the piston crown takes the form of a circular platform proud of the surface and entering the cylinder barrel. The clearance between it and the top of the rising piston is very small.

Each sparking plug is deeply recessed in a channel between the valves. On the compression stroke the mixture is swirled towards the plug with a high degree of turbulence, and a good flame-spread results. On the exhaust stroke the spent gases are similarly buffeted towards the exhaust valve, which ensures good scavenging.

As soon as carbon forms to any thickness it will begin to upset the fast flow of the gases and also increase the compression. This leads to pinking or detonation, becoming progressively more noticeable under conditions of load. Detonation takes the form of metallic rattling clearly audible above the slight noise of the engine.

The Decarbonizing Mileage. It is difficult to lay down firm rules about decarbonizing "by the clock" as engine performance is a much better guide. Generally at least 2,000 miles will be covered between decarbonizations, but the work is so simple that it can be undertaken as soon as the fine edge of performance begins to be lost.

Preliminary Dismantling. To prepare for the work put the machine on its stand and tackle whichever cylinder head is tilted downwards. With a ($\frac{1}{4}$) set spanner gently unscrew the drain plug from the bottom of the selected cylinder head. This plug is at the lowest point and distinguishable from the cylinder holding nuts by the absence of a screwed stud passing through it (*see* Fig. 3).

The plug is of brass and screws directly into the soft aluminium of the cylinder head. It must be handled very carefully. If roughly removed or replaced, and especially if overtightened, the screw thread in the aluminium will be damaged, making it difficult or impossible to ensure a watertight joint. Under the plug is a red fibre washer, another indication that it must not be over-tightened.

Arrange a space on the bench at least a foot square. If you have no bench, put a box lid or an old tray somewhere where it cannot be kicked over. This is to take the bits and pieces from the engine, neatly and in order. Put the drain plug there for a start. If the water does not flow freely, poke out the plug orifice with a spent match or a piece of wire so that the sludge or obstruction comes away.

Next slightly loosen the six $\frac{1}{4}$ BSF nuts holding the head. Take care over this too, loosening first the left centre, then the right centre, top left, bottom right, and so on in that or some order equally even. This done, the moment is convenient to alter the stance of the machine. While it is on its stand the engine cannot be turned over by the starting handle. Instead, then, chock the machine up by two blocks of wood or other solid supports, one under the footboard at each side. Then release the prop stand.

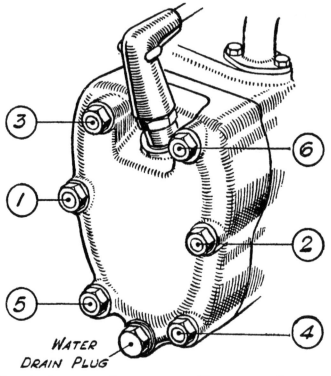

WATER
DRAIN PLUG

FIG. 9. ORDER OF LOOSENING OR TIGHTENING CYLINDER
HEAD SECURING NUTS

As mentioned before, post-1952 machines have independently-operated prop-stands and starting handles. These models can be started, or have their engines turned, while the prop-stand is down.

Taking the Head Off. Stand astride the machine, pull up the starting handle, and spin the engine briskly a couple of times. Keep an eye on the cylinder head receiving attention, and as the engine spins the head will be seen to loosen at once. Discreet tapping with a wooden or rawhide mallet is permissible (but should not normally be necessary).

Unscrew the six nuts in pairs from the cylinder head, and lay them on the bench or in the tray, arranged as they are fitted to the head, and letting each be placed upon its associated washer.

Any washer that sticks can be freed by a light tap from the edge of the spanner. Notice that nothing has been written so far about removing the sparking plug, which should be left where it is for the present. The oil filter (*see* Fig. 27) is eased out of the way.

Now with the fingers *and with nothing else* draw the cylinder head squarely off the six holding studs. As it comes away keep an eye on the gasket. It nearly always remains lightly stuck to the cylinder barrel and there it should be left for the present. If it sticks to the head and partly to the barrel, prise it carefully from the head with the fingers.

The author does not believe that gaskets should be renewed in all cases. On the contrary if they are in good condition it is better to replace existing gaskets since they have already been compressed and settled down.

Two Types of Gasket. LE 150 models were fitted at the factory with aluminium/asbestos gaskets. LE 200 models have "Plexeal" plastic gaskets. They can be used on 150 models but two gaskets have to be fitted to each joint (there is only one layer on the 200 model). At a casual glance the gaskets look symmetrical. Closer examination shows that they are not, and this makes it more than usually important for them to be put back the right way up.

New Plexeal gaskets must be "cooked" after fitting, and re-tightened. First fill only the engine water-jackets; run the engine until this water boils. Then carefully re-tighten the cylinder head nuts in the order suggested on page 12 (Fig. 9), afterwards fully re-filling the water system.

On 1965 LE models the cylinder heads and barrels, and of course gaskets, have been modified by displacement of the bottom water passage. Note that 1965 parts will fit earlier machines, and the makers describe as "no disadvantage" the slight masking of the waterways that results.

At this stage it is as well to digress for a moment to emphasize the wisdom of carrying through the decarbonizing operation with one cylinder at a time, reassembly and all. If both heads are removed at the same time and taken to the bench or place of work, the operator is certain to find great difficulty later in identifying which head is which. After dismantling the components it is better to mate up the same ones again.

Removing the Carbon. Stuff a piece of clean rag into the exposed cylinder bore to keep dirt out. Take the cylinder head to the bench or equivalent. Caution must be observed in removing carbon from an aluminium head, and the more it is crusted the greater the care needed. The metal is soft and the carbon hard.

The more the aluminium surface can be cleaned and burnished the less easy will it be for subsequent carbon formation to cling.

It is assumed that the reader has only ordinary hand equipment. It may be that he is so fortunate as to own, or be able to borrow, a small electric or air-driven rotary machine like a Wolf, Black and Decker, or Desoutter. If so, he can mount in the chuck a small pointed brass brush and with it buff the cylinder head combustion surfaces to mirror perfection.

More primitive non-scratch gear can be found in the form of an oak or other hardwood slip, a heavy stick of solder, or a bar of soft brass. Fashion a chisel edge on any of these and chip the carbon away with it. These soft tools can be used also on the piston top with the same safety as the head. At all costs avoid old screwdrivers, steel chisels and similar abominations. Sooner or later one's hand slips and there is a nasty, irremovable score in the aluminium.

Caustics are violent carbon looseners, all right with iron and steel but barred for aluminium and all lightweight alloys. If the carbon is really troublesome leave the part to soak overnight in a mixture of engine oil and paraffin.

Before working on the cylinder head, unscrew the sparking plug and lean it in the corner of a box, points upwards. Fill the interior of the plug with clean petrol. If an hour or two of this does not yield a reasonably clean plug the nearest garage with sand-blast equipment will scour both plugs for a few coppers. In this case thoroughly swill them out with petrol and leave to dry before refitting, to make sure no harmful sand particles can play havoc with the engine. The foregoing applies particularly to non-detachable plugs, and a short later chapter deals with the cleaning and resetting of the detachable variety.

The Piston and Valves. When the head is clean the top of the piston should be inspected. Take out the rag from the bore and rotate the engine until both valves are seen to close as the piston rises, that is, on the compression stroke. Carbon deposited round the valves and on their heads can then be cleaned away. By all means use the automatic buffing tool if available. Otherwise go gently to work with an old screwdriver, but on no account touch the piston top with it. Use only soft tools for this.

Do the valves need grinding? Turn the engine over slowly and the exhaust valve will open. Naturally it is always the dirtier of the two, which helps to identify it. It is, of course, the nearer to the exhaust port and pipe. It will open sufficiently for a fair appraisal of the state of the seating.

This is likely to be discoloured, but it is the presence of pits, that is blackened spots, on the bevelled edge that matters much more than darkening of the seat. It will help the examination to wash round the valve with petrol and a bristle brush. When it has been decided whether or not the exhaust valve must be ground-in, the engine should be turned over again and the same drill gone through with the inlet valve.

A much cleaner seating is sure to be found here, but again the final test is the presence or absence of pits. Contrary to former cherished beliefs it is not necessarily a good idea to disturb the valves every time an engine is decarbonized. This may have to be done if there is excessive carbon formation in the ports, which need not be anticipated at moderate mileages.

The rider, having decided to decarbonize, will know if the engine has felt woolly and lacking in compression when turned over on the starting handle. Such woolliness indicates that gas is leaking past the valves and that grinding-in is desirable.

Valve-grinding. The amateur is liable to do far more harm than good when he attacks his valves with grinding paste. It is often sold in tins containing coarse and fine grades, but a valve, especially such a small one as on the LE, is much better refaced if it will not clean up with fine paste, rather than assaulted by the brash amateur with the coarse variety. Equipment to grind the valves of an LE should include a little fine paste, a tool to grasp the valve during grinding, and a spring compressor (essential in order to remove the cotters without risk of damage).

Once again it is wise not only to deal with the one cylinder, on which work is in progress, at a time, but also to cope with one valve at a time and leave its fellow undismantled. Inlet and exhaust valves, and springs, are the same size. If only one is adrift at a time no undesirable interchanges can be made. Start with the exhaust, which is the harder work. Of different steel, it is identified by a small depression in the head (the inlet valve is flat-headed).

The cylinder barrel has to be taken off. First detach the exhaust and inlet pipes, being watchful that the nuts do not slip down inside. Next take off the cylinder barrel holding nuts, "patterning" them on the bench for later correct replacement. The barrel will now come off quite easily. Look out for the base gasket and try to leave it in position on the crankcase mouth. A hand should be ready underneath the cylinder while the other hand withdraws it, the free hand catching the piston and connecting-rod assembly to prevent them dropping down against the crankcase mouth.

The cylinder barrel can now be taken to the work-place with of course both valves, springs and so on, in position. With a spring compressor (buy or borrow one) compress the exhaust valve spring, remove the split cotters as they are exposed, and carefully release the compressor. The assembly now comes apart: valve, spring, and the cotters already removed with their collar. Set all but the valve to one side ready to put together again.

Clean the valve first of all carbon on the underside of the head and the stem. Make a note to pick out the deposit from within the port passage in the barrel prior to reassembly. To grind the valve either a rubber cup on a convenient rod is needed, to grip the head by suction, or a chuck tool to grip the stem at the other end. A light spring under the head is a help. Pick up a little well-mixed fine paste on the fingertip and smear it evenly round the valve seat. Slip the valve back in its guide with the suggested light spring under the head, press down (or pull down, depending on the tool used) rotate, release; repeat.

Good Valve-grinding. There is a trick about this and patience is the main secret. Press down with a light oscillating movement and constantly lift. Never screw it right round. Every three or four times redistribute the abrasive, replace, and oscillate again. After six or seven twists remove the valve, wash the head in petrol and minutely examine the seating. Stop grinding as soon as a matt grey line shows right round the seat.

If the pits do not readily disappear take the valve and the cylinder barrel to a dealer and have both refaced. Continued grinding to eliminate pits in the seating lowers the valve head into the seat and causes the valve opening to become partly masked by pocketing. If seat and head are refaced, metal is removed from both.

A thorough swabbing in petrol, or paraffin, of seat, ports, valve, and spring components, should precede refitting. It is extremely important to get rid of every trace of grinding paste. Before inserting the valve in its guide smear the stem with a little clean engine oil. The whole of the foregoing process is then repeated with the inlet valve.

The Piston and Rings. With both valves clean and gas-tight there remains only a check-over for the piston before the barrel is replaced. The three piston rings should be free in their grooves. They, and the outside of the piston, should present a uniformly polished appearance.

Brown burn marks extending down the piston skirt suggest one of two faults. Either the rings are defective and need renewal, or the cylinder bore is worn. In either case hot gases from the combustion chamber are finding their way past the "seal" and power is being lost. At under 10,000 miles the fault is almost certain to lie with the rings. At more than this mileage the advice of the dealer should be sought about reboring and the fitting of oversize pistons.

Sometimes, but seldom, one finds a broken ring. If this is so, fit a new set, and do not just renew the broken one. The old trick in removing or refitting piston rings of using three thin strips of metal as "shoehorns" makes the task easy without further breakages. Sound but discarded rings can be kept as emergency spares. One should be taken to the dealer for size in buying the new set. Before fitting the new rings to the piston, slide each individually into the lower part of the cylinder bore and hold it up to the light. A small but definite gap should be visible between the ends of the ring.

LE models have for some time been fitted with taper-faced chromium-plated top (or compression) rings. These are marked with the word "top" on the edge of the ring nearer to the piston head, so no mistake need be made in fitting. There is one of these taper rings to each piston.

If all is well slip the new rings on over the three tin strips. Of course fit first the bottom ring, the farthest away. Set the gaps at 120° away from each other to give the largest separation and longest path for any escaping gases, and while doing this make sure the rings rotate freely in their grooves.

Before the cylinder barrel is replaced feel the small-end bearing, or gudgeon-pin. This is the component securing the piston to the connecting-rod and though it should be quite free there must be no trace of play or shake. A similar test with the big-end bearing, securing the connecting-rod to the crankshaft, will probably show some slight side play. This is permissible, the LE up to late 1953 models having roller-bearing big-ends in which some play is inevitable.

Loose Bearings. If there is noticeable looseness at the big-end or any detectable movement at the gudgeon it would be a pity to reassemble without doing something about it and the dealer should be consulted. A new gudgeon-pin is relatively easy to fit but the big-end bearing is not normally accessible. Considerable dismantling is required but the engine should not be run with play in a big-end, as this means that play is likely also to be present in the main bearings.

Reassembling the Cylinder. If all is well, however, prepare to rebuild the cylinder by first getting everything scrupulously clean. Then smear the base surface of the cylinder barrel with grease: a thin continuous film. Check the gasket and if in good condition press it down upon the crankcase mouth (which can be coated with grease as with the cylinder base). Finally grease the outer surface of the gasket.

The cylinder bore should be lightly coated with engine oil. "Offer it," as the engineer would say, to the piston. Coaxing in the head of this is much helped by the chamfer on the inside of the barrel skirt. At the same time compress the rings with the free hand and slide the barrel on without turning it.

When it is in place screw down the base nuts with the fingers, putting them back, with their washers, upon the studs from which they were removed. When the spanner is used the nuts should be tightened gradually in a diagonal sequence, each a fraction only at a time. This care has to be observed even more particularly if a new gasket has been fitted.

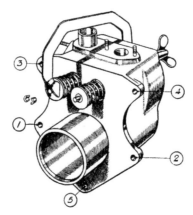

FIG. 10. VALVE COTTER REMOVAL AND ORDER OF TIGHTENING OF CYLINDER BASE SECURING NUTS

With the barrel firmly in position the valve clearances must be reset. There is a small oblong plate over each pair of tappets, held by four $\frac{1}{8}$ in. nuts. Remove this and rotate the engine until the piston rises on the compression stroke and both valves are closed. This is the right moment to adjust both valves. Take care not to confuse the piston position with that of the exhaust stroke, on which the piston is again rising but the exhaust valve almost immediately begins to open and a false reading will result. Turn the engine over several times if there is the slightest doubt that the correct moment has been reached.

Checking the Clearances. The LE 150 engine has square, non-rotating tappets, but those on the 200 model are of the orthodox round pattern, which rotate. The inlet is set to 0·004 in. and the exhaust to 0·006 in. Use undamaged feeler gauges to measure the clearances. Many people try to set valve clearances with bruised or torn gauge blades which may give a wrong indication.

On any model LE the valve clearances should receive one regular meticulous reset at each grinding, and not be the subject of constant tinkering.

3 Sparking plugs for the LE and Valiant

REGULAR attention in the LE models must be given to the sparking plugs, which are of the relatively unusual 10 mm type with long reach (12·5 mm). The correct patterns are Champion Z-10, K.L.G. Ten L30, NGK B-7H or Lodge CL10.* A shorter reach plug must *never* be used. As will be seen in a later chapter the generator spark gap is highly important and if wrongly set will impair engine performance. This performance equally depends upon clean and properly gapped sparking plugs, for the novel and ingenious engine layout is more sensitive to small variations in the ignition system than is the case with power units of greater size and more conventional design.

The chapter on decarbonizing contains a caution about the removal and refitting of the sparking and water drain plugs. The cylinder heads of the LE are of the soft metal aluminium, into which all these plugs are directly threaded. Rough handling quickly wears and destroys screw threads in this metal. The plug areas are water-jacketed, which keeps the plugs at a low working temperature and gives them a long life. It also means that if the threads in the head are damaged they cannot be bored out and bushed, so that if the plug threads are damaged beyond their ability to retain the plugs gas-tight, new cylinder heads must be fitted.

The plugs are easy of access, and their very readiness to hand may tempt the owner to use an adjustable spanner or some similar makeshift in removing them. A ring or box spanner is the proper tool. Another mistake is to over-tighten the sparking plugs. They should be run in with the fingers and the spanner finally applied to secure a light firmness little exceeding the tension applied by the fingers alone.

To be sure that this can be done clean their housings, threads and washers regularly with a clean petrol-moistened rag or soft brush. This avoids carrying bits of road grit into the threads, which quickly injures them and destroys the gas-tight fit. A smear of graphite grease on the threads is a good idea.

The 10 mm plug is small and rather less robust than the bigger types. The detachable variety can still be taken apart for cleaning. Non-detachable types should be cleaned on an air-blast unit provided at most garages (*see* page 110). The small dimensions preclude poking into the body to clear out carbon.

* *The Valiant twin (see page 58) uses the same types.*

19

Dismantling the Plug. Either use a proper plug-dismantling tool, or put the plug in a small vice, terminal upwards, gripping it lightly by the larger body-hexagon. It is quite easy to crush one of these plugs by screwing up the vice too heartily, which is why a small one should be used. Over the smaller hexagon, the top of the gland nut, slip a ring or box spanner. If a box spanner, use one that has neither sprung nor distorted.

Assume that a ring spanner is used, and that the operator is right-handed. The shank of the spanner should be parallel to the

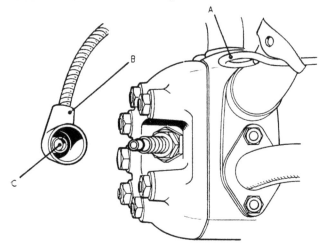

FIG. 11. PLUG CABLE TERMINAL

A = "Easy start" carburettor control.
B = H.T. cover.
C = Spring clip for sparking plug attachment.

vice jaws and pointing to the right. Hold the end firmly down over the gland nut with the left hand. "Bump" the heel of the right hand gently against the other end of the spanner until the nut yields. The object of this is to prevent the plug being forced out of the vice, or the spanner slipping off the gland nut, either of which mishaps will damage the plug.

Gland nut and core will come away together without separating. There is an internal copper washer of dished shape which may detach itself. It must be carefully watched for because without it the plug is not gas-tight and is therefore useless. Clean the soot off the porcelain core with a fine wire brush or emery paper, wash it in petrol, and lay it to one side.

Cleaning the Plug Casing. Take this out of the vice and scrape the interior with any convenient sharp metal strip thin enough to enter. The small blade of a penknife does very well. Get the casing quite clean within, wash it out with petrol, and finally scrub the L-shaped electrode or adjustable point with a fine wire brush till it is bright and clean.

The plug should be reassembled before any attempt can be made to reset the clearance. Smear the interior gland-nut thread and the dished copper washer with a thin coating of high-melting-point grease (sold under this description and sometimes known simply as H.M.P.). When screwing the interior back into position reverse the procedure already described for dismantling. Do not tighten violently. The plug will seal itself internally with the help of the H.M.P. grease.

The Plug Gap. The proper sparking plug gap for the LE engine is 20 thousandths of an inch.* Though this looks a large gap it is right and should not be reduced—the makers know best. Hold the plug at eye level against the light and see that the feeler gauge slips fairly stiffly between the points. If the plug has had a fair amount of use look closely to see that there is not a false gap due to uneven burning of the electrodes.

Remember the oft-repeated caution—never try to bend the centre electrode. For those who take real trouble with their plugs a plug regapping tool is available. Verify finally that the ring washer (copper/asbestos) on the outside of the plug is in good condition. It does not matter if this is flattened, but fit a new one if it is bruised or split.

The insulated suppressor caps are a press fit over the special waisted nipple screwed on the plug top. Periodically give the insulated caps a firm push down, for mysterious bad running can often be traced to a thing as simple as a terminal that has jumped off though the cap still remains apparently in position.

Appearance of the Points. A plug functioning correctly will always have a slightly sooty appearance except at the points themselves. These develop a light biscuit colour if the mixture is correct and the spark good. Blackened plugs are associated with lumpy running and a tendency to engine stoppage in traffic. This may be due to insufficient low-speed air—*see* the air-bleed paragraph, page 41.

Slight unevenness in running should not be confused with the effect produced by fixed ignition on early LE models. The spark on these is set at full advance, and a slow smooth tickover cannot be expected on these machines as with later types because such a tickover is produced by a partly retarded spark. A further reference to this matter is made in the chapter on ignition and generators.

* *The makers' actual latitude is* 0·018–0·023 *in.*

It is wise to buy and carry two new plugs, which should be kept protected in the maker's wrappings. Velocette dealers always have the correct long-reach type, but the only 10 mm plug stocked

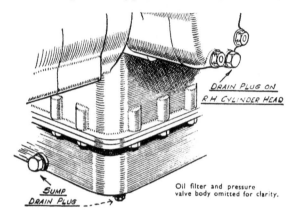

FIG. 12. ENGINE SUMP DRAIN PLUG
Dotted arrow shows position on earlier models.

by most small cycle-shops is the short-reach variety used by many cyclemotors. The LE is designed for the 12·5 mm (long-reach) type.

Lubrication: the Oil Filter. The owner-rider of the LE need bother little about lubrication other than to watch the level of the engine sump oil (1¾ pints), and at long intervals to make sure there is still a quarter pint of heavy oil in both gearbox and final drive (*see* Figs. 3 and 19). Additive oils are not recommended. Where a Tecalemit oil filter is fitted the cartridge filter must be extracted and renewed every 10,000 miles.

On no account should any attempt be made to clean the sludge from the cartridge and use it again. Throw it away and fit a new one. If this is done at every eighth engine oil change the interior of the engine will be kept in the best possible condition.

This filter-and-oil change is a perfectly straightforward operation but somewhat messy. One should therefore put a large tin tray under the engine to catch the drips.

4 Ignition and Generators (LE and Valiant)

IGNITION and lighting are provided in all LE models by a battery, and a generator driven off the front end of the crankshaft. The generator protrudes immediately below the radiator and is quite accessible. On models up to and including 1964, the battery was of 6 volt, 8 amp size. Police models retain this, but 1965 LEs and Vogues have 12-volt batteries.

A good light is the first essential if any work is to be done on the generator, and a hand lamp or torch will be needed at some time during the operation. A second essential is for the operator to get himself and the machine into the right relative positions to tackle the job as easily and as comfortably as possible. Ideally the machine should be run up on a ramp and the steering put on full right lock and secured there with a chunk of wood or by lashing the handlebars.

However, the operator can manage at ground level with the machine on its stand. One needs to sit facing the generator end-cover with the front wheel by the right shoulder.

THE B.T-H. GENERATORS

The PEC Generator. LE 150s and some Mk. IIs were fitted with this. The end cover is retained by four small nuts and lock-washers so one must first remove these and put them safely aside. The bottom nut also retains the earth wire and the rubber overflow pipe from the radiator. Push the wire out of the way and poke the tube behind a legshield.

The pressed-steel cover is a tight fit, and the generator body is of vulcanite. Incorrect removal of the cover can cause chipping or fracture. At the lowest point of the cover there is a lip, set backwards, like the lip on a polish tin. If a small square of hard-wood is placed against this lip and given a couple of taps with a tack-hammer the cover will disengage easily. It should not be prised off.

The Contact-Breaker. This is now exposed, the points and condenser being seen at the bottom centre. Most likely it will be the points that the operator wishes to check. The moving point can be pulled down with the left thumb, and the hand torch suggested earlier plus perhaps a small mirror will make it possible to see the surfaces of both points. Those accustomed to the use of watchmakers' lenses will find that one of these is a considerable help.

Various methods of cleaning burned points are: using a carborundum slip, a magneto file, or a piece of fine emery cloth wrapped round a nail file so that there is an abrasive surface each side. Press the points together upon the cleaning medium and rub lightly, inspecting the result at frequent intervals.

This is a tedious business in an awkward position and it may take half an hour or more to get the points bright and square.

When the burnishing seems to be adequate and the points close reasonably square against each other clean up all round them and their mountings with a small soft brush and a few drops of petrol. Get rid of every trace of emery, especially between the points. Apart from its abrasive nature a single grain left unnoticed here, or indeed any minute particle of foreign matter, will completely prevent a spark occurring.

Checking the Gap. This too is a tricky and tedious process. The gap must be precise, and a false reading is all too easy to get. The PEC generator is extremely sensitive to the gap size, which must be small: 0·012 in. A feeler gauge is included in the generator and will be found immediately beneath the "3 o'clock" cover bolt, sprung into a recess. If it is missing, get a replacement from the B.T-H. company at Rugby.

To Adjust the Gap. The early LE must be taken off its stand and chocked up with a block about 4 in. thick underneath each footboard. This is because the model can only have the engine rotated via the starting handle.* Make sure the cycle is secure, though it can lean over slightly to the near side with some advantage, the off-side block remaining in position for safety's sake. Take out the sparking plugs so that the engine can be turned over slowly without effort.

Reset the steering, wedging it on full right lock, and resume the former seated position by the front wheel. Verify that it is possible to reach up with the left arm and push the engine round on the starting handle, very slowly.

The large cam, right at the centre of the generator, turns in a clockwise direction with the crankshaft, so causing the half-speed fibre distributor wheel above it to rotate anti-clockwise. There is a small flat on the cam which permits the points to close for about one-third of each rotation. This can be seen as the engine is slowly pushed round. The rise or "bump" on the cam strikes the fibre heel of the moving point, and displaces it, at about "7 o'clock."

* *See also pages* 1, 56.

When this occurs, slip the gauge between the points, where it should be retained. Give another half-inch of circular rotation on the cam, taking the moving point to the moment of maximum separation. If the gauge falls out the gap is too wide. It should stay put. Check, in this case, for too small a gap.

The fixed, adjustable, point is retained by two large screws seen between the points and the condenser. Loosen the upper screw a little, and then the lower, just enough to permit movement when gentle leverage is applied against the mounting plate, on the appropriate side, with the tip of the screwdriver. By "appropriate" is meant to close or widen the gap according to whether the feeler gauge showed this to be wide or too narrow. It will be seen that the lower screw covers a short slot while the upper screw acts as a pivot. Hence if they are only slightly loosened the adjustable point will not slip about when the pressure is removed.

"Fixed" and "Moving" Points. The *moving* point pivots about a pin and is pressed by the cam away from the fixed point against the resistance of a double spring blade, there being a short keeper blade to damp the spring movement. This point, though the moving component, cannot be moved in the other sense, that of adjustment of position to vary the gap size.

The *fixed* point, on the other hand, is a simple affair retained by its two screws in one position during the running of the engine. For the operation of regapping, and only at this time, the fixed point is moved so that it may be reset to give the correct gap. If the operator is still a little confused about this, the points should be watched closely while the engine is turned round a few times. The relative movement of the spring point will then be clear.

If the blade is a sliding fit at the moment of maximum separation just described, the gap is correct. The trouble is that, however delicately one works, it is difficult to retighten the retaining screws without disturbing the adjustment. And they must be quite tight, or the impact of the moving point will instantly derange the gap. Leave the blade between the points while each screw is gingerly tightened.

Even when it appears that success is achieved the gap should be rechecked at a number of places round the proud (projecting) area of the cam. Finally turn the engine over again and recheck.

One essential for good work is a sound screwdriver. Best of all is a first-class ratchet job such as a Yankee or Millers Falls. With this tool a steady pressure can be exerted on the screw head, minimizing slipping and the tell-tale amateur trademark of burred slots. Therefore go to a good toolshop and choose a screwdriver about 6 in. long. Ask the assistant to grind a parallel tip on it. Most screwdrivers have a chisel or taper tip which greatly increases the risk of slipping. A parallel tip will fit closely in the screw slot without budging.

Retiming. This is a skilled job for the dealer and one which requires a special tool to remove the cam from the end of the crankshaft.

Furthermore, as mentioned in the chapter on sparking plugs, some LE models have fixed timing. On these machines the automatic mechanism, contained within the cam, is pinned to render it inoperative, the spark being set to occur somewhat before T.D.C. piston position. This corresponds to full advance. Machines with automatically variable timing are of course timed with the mechanism at rest, on full retard. As it is not easy to recognize which type of cam is fitted, adjustment of the timing without this essential knowledge could result in damage to the engine.

Keeping the Generator Clean. The interior mechanism of the B.T-H. generator is readily kept clean. The tight-fitting cover-plate will prevent dirt entering, but too generous lubrication will cause interior fouling. If any carbon dust is present, remove it with a soft dry brush.

Therefore confine oiling and greasing to the following. Each time the points are set—normally at intervals of some thousands of miles—put one drop of fine machine oil on the pivot of the moving point, where an inner wick will retain it. Rub a trace of H.M.P. grease on the fibre heel, to ease its passage on the cam face. Excess of either oil or grease will soon find its way on to the surfaces of the points, with disastrous results to the spark.

Renewing the Points. After a considerable mileage the points may deteriorate to an extent where it is better to renew them than to waste time trying to stone them flat. Also when a lot of tungsten has been ground away it is difficult or impossible to set the gap properly. To remove the moving point have available a magneto spanner to take the spring blade off the end of the condenser—on no account use pliers for this—and a pair of long-nosed pliers *only* for the purpose of dismantling the pivot bearing.

Remove the nut and washer from the end of the condenser and at once put these in a safe place with the short check-spring on the outside of the longer bow-spring connecting the condenser to the moving point. Slip this bow-spring off and leave it free. The check-spring may be found fitted underneath the bow-spring, which some experts consider to be the correct position (in this case the bent end faces away from the longer spring).

As will be seen, the moving point pivots on a small pin. At the top of this pin, nearest to the operator, is a minute spring circlip or C-washer. It is necessary to find the two adjacent ends of this circlip and by pressing them towards the pin to spring the clip open so that it can be pulled out of the groove in which it is located. Use the long-nosed pliers with the index finger of the left hand pressed lightly over the end of the pin to prevent the circlip leaping out and becoming lost.

Once the circlip, which is extremely small, has been captured the best thing is to put it right out of the way in a tin lid with a blob of grease on it to keep it prisoner. Its loss immobilizes the whole machine. Underneath the circlip is a plain washer, almost as small, and it too should go in the tin lid.

The moving point now draws off and can be laid aside. The fixed point follows. It is retained by the two adjustment screws, the lower of which also retains the condenser in place. Take away this lower screw with its spring washer, and out comes the condenser. By the way a spare condenser is an extremely handy spare to carry and one which only costs a few shillings. Removal of the upper screw and washer completes dismantling and both points are now available.

If they are in poor shape fit a new pair forthwith. If there is still plenty of tungsten they can be worked up with a slip, obtainable from accessory firms, made like the emery board of a manicure set. To do the job scientifically screw the fixed point by woodscrews through its fixing holes to a flat piece of wood. With a long woodscrew secure the moving point through its pivot hole to the board, both points thus being in the same relative positions as they occupy in the generator.

Stoning the Points. They are now in the proper position to be stoned. Press them lightly together with the left finger and thumb and hold the stoning slip between them. Rub the slip lightly and slowly to and fro. At frequent intervals inspect the work. Obvious as the caution may sound, do not make the mistake that many impatient amateurs make of trying to tear off all the bad metal in about two strokes. Be prepared to spend half an hour on the job.

When they look square and clean, replace the stoning slip with a fold of *worn* 00 emery cloth wrapped round both surfaces of the slip. This is to burnish the surfaces of the points and is again done slowly to and fro, with light pressure. Periodically inspect the result with that useful jeweller's eyeglass, which reveals a ridged coarse surface where the eye appears to detect perfection. The points when finished should appear like mirrors under the eyeglass.

Though most electricians declare for two dead flat surfaces on the points, abutting squarely on each other, some urge that the points are better finished slightly convex. This result can be obtained by ignoring the board and screw method and instead mounting the flat side of a chip of oilstone in a hand brace. Put the side grip of the brace in a vice, turn the wheel with the right hand and in turn offer each point to the flat oilstone chip, using the lightest possible pressure. If the points are finished in this way the emery polishing is not needed.

Whichever method is used the points must be finally washed in petrol and dried.

Remounting the Points. Reverse the sequence just described. If the check-spring is mounted first on the end of the condenser its bent end should point away from the main spring. When the moving point is replaced on its pivot the circlip will be found much easier to put back than it was to remove. The small flat washer first goes on top of the point bearing. Then the circlip can be picked up on the fingertip with a trace of grease. Press the clip firmly down over the pin and it will snap into place. Finally use the tips of the long-nosed pliers to position it definitely within its groove.

Lastly the points have to be reset as described earlier. The whole of the foregoing holds good, of course, with slight variations, for the points of any type of ignition device including the Miller AC to be described later.

Removing the Bakelite Wheel. Before leaving the B.T-H. there remain the coil and the distributor pinion to be verified for cleanness. First the distributor; the large upper gear wheel, of Bakelite, should be examined closely. The roots of two adjacent teeth have fine white dots marked upon them. Turn the engine until these are vertically downwards and it will be found that they mesh with one of the teeth on the steel pinion having a dot punched on it. Before removing the Bakelite pinion these three teeth should always be thus in mesh. *Do not therefore turn the engine again until the present operation is complete.*

Upon the centre of this pinion a spring blade presses. The other end of the spring blade is retained under a bolt within a fitted recess at the top of the black tubular high-tension coil. Unscrew this bolt and the spring will come away. Nothing else retains the Bakelite wheel, which can now be lifted off.

Wipe it over with a petrol-damped rag and dry the wheel thoroughly. On the underside there is a metal distributor finger, a "jump-spark" device. If this is roughened at the end, where the spark occurs, smooth the roughness away with a piece of worn emery cloth. The round hole immediately over the end of the finger is for inspection purposes so that when it is in position its approach to the two high-tension contacts can be seen and checked.

These contacts are respectively at the "3 o'clock" and "9 o'clock" positions, one for each cylinder. They are unlikely to present a badly burned appearance and can be touched up with emery and afterwards carefully cleaned.

Remember in putting back the pinion to get the punched dot between two white ones, otherwise the timing will be deranged and the engine will not start. The spring blade must press firmly on the centre of the wheel—if not fit a new blade—and the contact must be clean and bright. The efficiency of the sparks depends on this.

If there seems to be any deposit of dirt on the high-tension coil the small amount of trouble involved in removing it, wiping it over, and replacing it, would be well repaid. If the surface of the coil is filmed with dirt the current can leak away. There is no adjustment on the coil, which either works or does not. It is held by two screws.

The PEC generator has another function to perform, that of a dynamo. The dynamo mechanism is behind the steel pinion recently under inspection in these pages. Maintenance of this dynamo will not be touched upon in this book, since commutator and brush overhaul are beyond the skill of the ordinary layman. So much damage can be done to electrical apparatus by inexpert tinkering that it is at all times best to leave dynamo maintenance to the skilled electrician.

What the Dynamo Does. There will, however, be many who do not understand the dynamo's function at all. Its purpose is to charge the battery, so that the lights will be bright and the horn efficient, as well as the ignition being able to produce a hot spark. Symptoms that the dynamo requires attention are, first, a weak battery: feeble horn, poor lights. In this case the charge is perhaps insufficient. Second, the opposite state of affairs: strong lights and possibly bulbs burning out prematurely, coupled with gassing from the battery—excessive "fizzing"—and cheesy corrosion round the terminals, are indications of excessive charge from the dynamo. Any of these symptoms call for a visit to the expert.

The Cut-out. This is another item calling for no interference. The cut-out is found within the lower right side of the casing, beneath the slot in which you should wisely have replaced the valuable 0·012 in. feeler gauge (did you?). The small square casing houses an entirely automatic switch "making" or "breaking" the circuit to the battery. The cut-out operates as the current rises or falls above or below the minimum value necessary for charging, and prevents the battery discharging through the dynamo windings. Never tinker with it.

Replacing the Generator Cover. Before doing this, clean up generally with a petrol-damped rag. Wipe round the ledge or rim upon which the casing abuts. Read over the instructions printed on the inner face of the cover and check thereby that everything is in order. Swill the fixing nuts and washers in petrol, clean their threads and brush those of the bolts upon which they engage. Smear these with a trace of grease to make them easy to remove next time.

Press the cover evenly home. Replace the "earth" connexion at the lowest fixing point and resecure the rubber overflow water pipe. Water from the overflow must not be allowed to drip on to the generator casing. Tighten the fixing nuts evenly but not excessively.

THE MILLER GENERATORS

There are three types of these. The AC–3 is found on LE 200 machines (not 150 models) up to and including engine number 200/15839. Serial numbers 200/15840 upwards have the later type AC–3P instrument. Small but important differences exist between the two types and will be explained shortly. Thirdly there is the AC4, as used on the Mk. III (and Valiant) giving 42 watts.

It has been seen that the B.T-H. unit is a dynamo and coil ignition generator. The Miller of all types combines coil ignition with flywheel magnets energizing low-tension lighting coils, perhaps more accurately called charging coils. These generate alternating current which is rectified by a metal disc of special construction bolted, in models up to the 1954 series, beneath the petrol tank. The latest LE models have the rectifier housed on the offside within the lower part of the frame "backbone."

AC–3 Generators. These were used in conjunction with the same arrangement of switch panel, at the top of the right-hand legshield, as in the B.T-H. type PEC. The left-hand switch controls the lights and the right-hand one the ignition. Once again there is an emergency position marked on the right-hand switch. Turning the switch to the *left* cuts the battery out of circuit if this component is discharged or temporarily absent. The engine can then be started, and used at speeds not exceeding 30 m.p.h. When the switch is moved over to the normal "start" position (*right*) the battery is brought into circuit and the red light gives warning of this.

The AC–3P instrument has a circuit-breaker, as it is called. This has a particularly valuable function, operative if the battery should be wrongly replaced in its holder. If this were done the negative terminal would be, incorrectly, connected to "earth" and on the earlier AC–3 instrument this could result in the current, flowing the wrong way through the low-tension coils, demagnetizing the flywheel magnets. If this wrong connexion is made on the AC–3P the circuit-breaker at once breaks the circuit.

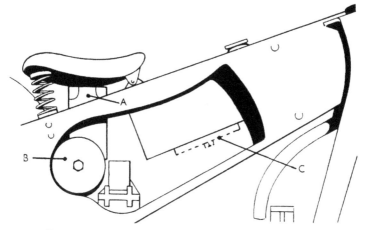

FIG. 13. POSITIONS OF THE RECTIFIER LE 200
(FRAME SHOWN CUT AWAY)

A = Battery.   B = Rectifier (1954 on).
C = Rectifier (pre-1954).

The AC–4 Generator. Fitted to the LE Mk. III and the Valiant, this uses a full-wave rectifier and gives higher output. Otherwise it resembles the earlier Miller instruments.

Batteries on all models must be connected with the *positive* terminal (marked with a red +) wired to frame or "earth." This should be most carefully checked whenever the battery is lifted out of its cradle underneath the saddle.

The right-hand switch panel, at the top of the legshield, takes a different form on most LE 200 models. There is no longer a red warning light, and an ammeter is fitted at the left side of the panel in place of the former light switch. The black turn-switch at the right side has six positions: *park, emergency, off, charge and ignition, head and tail*, and *pilot and tail*. A removable key engages a slot in the head of the switch, acting as an anti-thief device by enabling it to be left in the *off* (no lights) or *park* (pilot and tail)

positions. On the Mk. III up to 1965, instruments and switches
are mounted in the headlamp shell. For 1965 and later models
(12 V) they revert to the legshield panel.

The amateur owner whose machine is fitted with one of the
AC instruments need only be concerned with the gap at the points
and the general cleanness of the machine. The cover is removable
in the same way as with the B.T.-H. generator save that in the
Miller only two fixing nuts are used.

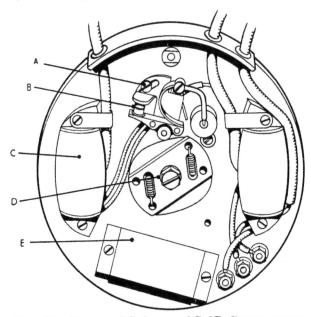

FIG. 14. MILLER AC–3 AND AC–3P GENERATORS

A = Screw retaining the fixed point.   D = Timing unit.
B = Points.   E = Circuit-breaker (AC-3P only).
C = Low-tension coil.

(The AC–4 generator is similar but is designed to work with a full-wave
rectifier.)

The Stator and Coils. These are found beneath the cover, the
stator being an aluminium casting. Mounted on it are the low-
tension coils at "3 o'clock" and "9 o'clock," the circuit-breaker, if
one is fitted, at "7 o'clock," the automatic timing unit at the
centre, and the points above and to the left of this.

Adjustment of the points is simplified by the single slotted
screw at roughly "11 o'clock" which is loosened to free the fixed
point. The gap can be verified by using a 0·015 in. feeler blade.
At maximum opening the gauge should be a tight sliding fit in
the gap. The setting is critical and should not be guessed.

Detailed instructions have been given earlier in this chapter about cleaning and trueing the points, and lubricating the

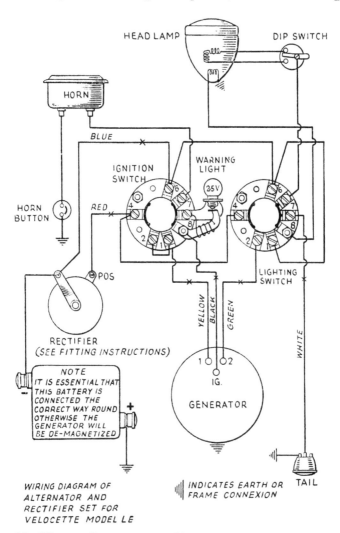

FIG. 15. WIRING DIAGRAM FOR MILLER AC-3 GENERATOR (6 V)
(Used on machines prior to Eng. No. 200/15840.)

machine. The same remarks apply to the Miller. In general the amateur is best advised to confine his work on the points to a polish with fine and worn emery cloth. Most damage to the points can be prevented because it generally occurs through grease getting burned into them. Instructions are given to grease the

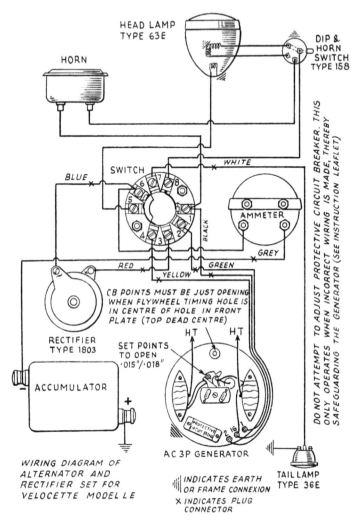

FIG. 16. WIRING DIAGRAM FOR MILLER AC–3P GENERATOR (6 V)
(Used on machines after Eng. No. 200/15840.)

cam pad each 2,000 miles, but this should not be done in such a way that there is a dab of grease left where it wanders about and eventually creeps over the points.

The Gap Narrows. Servicing of the points is more likely to be intelligently carried out if one realizes what tends to happen in

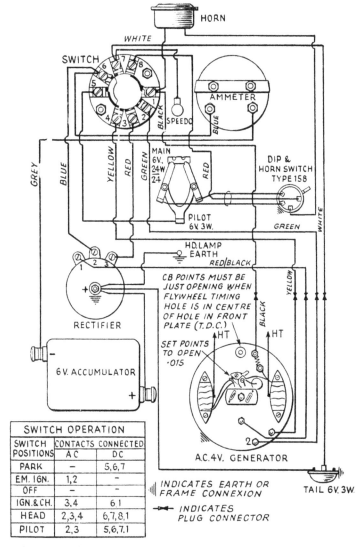

FIG. 17. WIRING DIAGRAM FOR MILLER AC–4 GENERATOR
(Used on LE Mk III machines and on Valiant models.)

the course of time. This is the slow process of wear on the cam heel, so that the gap tends to close very gradually. Too small a gap is a cause of intermittent misfiring when pulling uphill. This in time will foul the plugs. A small gap gives slightly easier starting and does not affect performance over the "pottering" range. Too large a gap makes starting hard but gives a good spark at full power.

The Battery. This is carried under the saddle (*see* Fig. 13). Add, about once a fortnight, enough distilled water to bring the liquid over the tops of the plates. A hydrometer is convenient for this and for testing as well.

If the Varley unspillable battery is used (as it generally is on this model) topping-up is still essential but should be very carefully done. The absorbent spongy material is kept saturated by adding distilled water, but avoid excess—add the water quite slowly.

The Varley can still be read by hydrometer if the nozzle of this instrument is pushed gently into the sponge material.

Changing Lamp Bulbs. For police machines and other 6-volt models, release the screw at the base of the headlamp front, when the reflector-rim unit can be eased off. Prise aside the two spring clips retaining the bulb-holder; this withdraws, giving access to the small parking light (6 V, 6 W, MES) and the main bulb (6 V, 24/24 W, BPF). For this a 30/30 W can be substituted if running is mainly by day.

The tail lamp (release plastic case) and pull-out miniature speedometer bulbs are 6 V, 3 W, SCC and 6·5 V, 0·195 W, bayonet-type respectively. Carry a set of spare bulbs in a proper case.

12-volt Electrics. The LE Mk. III, 1965 on, has a 12-V Lucas alternator rated at 90/100 W. A Zener Diode automatic voltage control, with a heat-sink bolted beneath the glove compartment, regulates the charge to twin Lucas 6-V, 8 A-h batteries type MKZ9E. The headlamp bulb becomes a 12-V, 50/40 W.

Other Lucas equipment includes twin ignition coils mounted behind the carburettor, feeding the sparking plugs through suppressor leads and normal insulated terminal covers.

5 The LE Petrol System

PETROL in all LE models is carried in a flat tank housed within the centre girder of the frame. Early models hold $1\frac{1}{4}$ gal, later increased to $1\frac{5}{8}$ gal ($7\frac{1}{2}$ l.). The tank and its pipe are so arranged that gravity feed will continue to function on any gradient that the machine will climb. Consumption, it will be remembered, is about 100 m.p.g. on the 150 models and 95 m.p.g. on the 200s. The Vogue model has a $2\frac{1}{2}$ gal tank (3 U.S., $11\frac{1}{3}$ l.) and similar consumption.

The tank cannot be removed without dismantling the cycle. It can, however, be completely emptied through the fuel line. Elaborate precautions are taken on all models to prevent foreign matter reaching the carburettor, but if water or bits of rust. rubber from the filling hose, or other debris, gets in the tank, it is not easy to eliminate. Water is a particular bugbear and one drop of rain falling in the tank can cause much trouble. It is worth while always to fill up under cover, and once a year, to flush out the tank.

Flushing the Tank. The flexible pipe from the tank to the carburettor can be detached and a couple of feet of plastic tubing temporarily substituted can lead the discharge out to a tin. If half a gallon of fuel is then poured into the tank it will bring away any foreign matter as it runs through.

A little pressure can be contrived in a variety of ways, from the blowing nozzle of a vacuum cleaner to the tyre air-line at the garage. Wrap any piece of clean dust-free cloth round the business end and press it down on the filling orifice of the tank, putting the pressure on in spurts. This will expel blobs of water which otherwise tend to remain in the outlet pipe.

In emergency an intermittent obstruction is easily cleared by pulling the filter bowl momentarily aside. If petrol does not flow freely the obstruction is in the pipe. A vigorous blast from the air-line will effect an instant cure. In isolated failures the tyre pump flex will do the trick. Remember, however, that some obstruction probably still remains within the tank and resolve to flush or blow it out, as detailed above, as soon as possible.

Conditions of heat or hard pulling on steep hills in second or first gears, particularly when carrying a pillion passenger, may cause the LE engine to die away through a fuel lock in the pipe. This too can be cleared by temporarily removing the filter bowl and blowing if the fuel does not flow freely. It will save a lot of futile tinkering if one remembers that on this machine trouble with the fuel feed is much more likely to occur before than after the very efficient petrol filter.

On early LE models the fuel line screws on to a petrol tap integral with the carburettor. Thus, if one wants to disconnect the carburettor while there is petrol in the tank, some fuel will be lost before a finger can be put over the end of the pipe. Later models have the tap in the end of the fuel line and separate from the carburettor.

At the point where the fuel first enters the carburettor it flows into a metal bowl held by a spring clip. Here it rises to pass through a filter medium and so into the float chamber of the carburettor itself. An all-metal "edge filter" was used on early models but this has been superseded by a felt cylinder on a stiffening base of wire mesh. The clip should be sprung off from time to time and the bowl washed out with petrol. The felt is retained by a brass nut and washer and if this too is taken off and given a bath in petrol no jet-stopping material should be able to pass into the carburettor.

The Air Filter. This further protects the jets. The air intake is led through a large rubber hose communicating with a fabric bag housed in a metal can with louvred sides fixed in the centre of the radiator.* Incoming air is thus both cleaned and warmed. The air hose is a push fit and in very dusty conditions some fine grit may eventually seep into the air intake.

If this occurs it can cause a partial or complete jet stoppage, popping-back in the carburettor or engine failure. The makers suggest that if such obstruction takes place but is not such as to stop the engine altogether it can be cleared in the following manner. Pull the hose off the intake and start the engine. Run this fairly fast, and intermittently poke a finger into the carburettor air intake. This will of course tend to stop the engine, and the finger should be removed before the engine dies out. Repeated two or three times this may cause the obstruction to be sucked out of the jets.

Dismantling the Carburettor. This becomes necessary if the jets will not clear themselves. First shut off the petrol by pushing the tap outwards. On early 150 models unscrew the union nut to the *right* of the tap and as quickly as possible transfer the fuel line

---

* *Not fitted to models having the Amal 363 monobloc carburettor.*

(from which petrol is now flowing) to a clean gallon tin. On all later models the union nut is to the *left* of the tap and the disconnexion is performed without loss of fuel. Remove the easy-start pull-rod from the rubber clip round the nearside water hose.

At the offside of the machine the throttle wire will be seen to be held by a small brass pinch-bolt. Use a small (3 in.) adjustable spanner rather than pliers to release this. The throttle wire can then be pulled out and removed with its outer covering. This completes the external attachments which must be dismantled from the carburettor.

This is held by a pinch-ring at the centre of the arched inlet manifold. Using the small adjustable spanner loosen the bolt on the pinch-ring until the union is free and the carburettor can be drawn off forward.

Take the carburettor to the bench. Again with the small adjustable spanner remove first the four fastening bolts underneath the jet block. Lay these out in a safe place with their lock washers, "patterning" them so that each can later be replaced in its correct socket. Next take off the two staggered nuts and washers that hold the triangular plate forming the anchorage for the throttle return spring. Note which way round this is fitted and no confusion will arise later when it has to go back. Leave the anchor plate to dangle from the spring.

Underneath the plate two more nuts will be found. These are really bolt-heads and when unscrewed they bring away with them the studs still holding the jet-block in position. Pull this carefully away from the body of the carburettor. There is a fibre gasket between them and some care is needed not to tear this.

Looking down on the jet-block the screw-cut heads of the four jets are now exposed, and the most delicate part of the operation follows. They are of different sizes and should on no account be all removed at once. Take one out at a time, using a fine screwdriver in good condition. At the bottom of the jet block is a small set-screw for the base of each jet and each having a small red fibre washer under it. Take out only the screw corresponding to the jet removed.

Cleaning the Jets. An air-line blast is the best jet and passage clearer. In default, the cycle pump may be used. Blow the jet through from the slotted end. Good sight is needed to see if the small aperture is really clear and a watchmaker's glass helps greatly. It is really not much use blowing through these jets with the mouth and one may simply reblock them by leaving a bead of saliva inside! Neither is it wise to poke a bit of wire through, which may upset the calibration of the jet. An obstinate block-up can sometimes be eased by a poke from a fine bristle, but the garage air-line is by far the best answer. Blow, too, right through the fuel passage from the float chamber.

As each jet is cleared it and its associated base plug should be screwed back. To be quite sure about the fuel passages it will be best to take the top off the float chamber and remove the float. The top is held by two large bolts, and the fibre washer between the top and the body must be preserved undamaged. Do not take it off the lid, to which it will probably stick tightly.

Air-bleed and Float. There are two fine air-bleed holes disposed horizontally in the edge of the float chamber lid. Mysterious troubles will occur if these become obstructed, so they should be found and poked through with a pin. (These are not jets and so it will not matter if they are slightly enlarged.) In lifting out the float be watchful not to bend the fine brass spindle protruding from it top and bottom. Memo for replacement; the pointed end must be uppermost as it controls the flow of petrol into the float chamber.

Any slight difficulty about clearing the jet passages is now greatly simplified. Shine a bright light into the empty float chamber, shield the eyes, and it will be possible to look through the fine passages from the float chamber to the jets.

In removing and replacing the jets remember that they are hard brass and most vulnerable to the screwdriver blade. If small flakes of brass are knocked off the slots they will go straight into the jet orifices and the last state will be worse than the first, because being of brass and relatively heavy, these fragments will tend to lodge firmly.

Jet Sizes. These are laid down with great insistence by the makers, who have been at pains to select them after long experiment. For the 150 model they are as follows: starting 15, pilot 30, main 20, compensator 25. No advantage is to be gained by altering any of these whether premium or commercial grade fuels are used.

For the 200 models sizes are: starting 20, pilot 25, main 25, compensator 20. Common to all carburettors are the three spray tubes, two inclined and stamped 145 and one vertical 25. Some early models had a 20 here and it is recommended that this be changed for a 25. The spray tubes are found not in the jet block but in the body of the carburettor above the jets, where they pass into the throat of the choke tube. Though they are unlikely to become obstructed it should be part of the routine to ensure that they are clear.

The Pilot Air-bleed. Apart from the throttle this is the only variable control on the carburettor. It is alongside the point at which the throttle cable is attached to the block and has a knurled spring-loaded setting knob. If a mark is scratched across the head of the knob one can more easily tell where one is when adjusting it. Optimum setting, determined by adjusting it in conjunction with the throttle-stop screw, is between two and three turns unscrewed from complete closure. Start therefore to adjust it by fully closing it and then turning back two full turns.

Dismantling the Air-cleaner. The bag of the air-cleaner needs a periodical clean, more so if much dust is encountered. The louvred metal enclosing can has a split edge round which there fits a retaining wire clip tightened with a wing nut. Do not entirely remove this, but loosen it enough to permit the can being slipped off the flange at the radiator centre. Pull out the fabric bag and, if very dirty, wash it in petrol or even in soapy water. Rinse and dry thoroughly.

Refitting is a little tricky. First slip the edge of the bag evenly over the flange in the radiator cell. Then, with the wire clip as loose as possible, work the louvred can over the bag and flange. If there are puckers or gaps unfiltered air will be drawn in. Work the wire ring down to the edge of the can and tighten securely.

Replacing the Carburettor. There is a minor snag about this which calls for special care. The instrument is simple to remove and would be equally so to replace were it not for the great importance of having the float chamber absolutely vertical in relation to the induction pipe. There are various ways of ensuring this and it is not important which the reader adopts. The simplest is to remove the induction pipe, fit the carburettor accurately to this, and then remount the two in one piece.

The induction pipe comes away when four $\frac{1}{8}$ in. bolts, two each side retaining the flanges, are removed. Take off the fastening nuts and washers and put to one side. Lift the pipe up, keeping an eye on the flange washers, which are important to preserve an airtight joint at each side. As soon as the pipe is out of the way stuff clean rag into each exposed port. It is very easy to drop small objects such as the fastening nuts and washers into the ports. If this happens there will be nothing for it but partially to dismantle the engine to recover them.

Within the induction stub at the centre of the pipe there should be a round felt washer. Check that this is so, and push the carburettor on to the stub. Tighten the pinch-bolt just enough to keep the two firmly together. The pipe with the carburettor in position can now be placed, resting on the flanges, on a level surface such as a table top.

With a set-square or some other vertical object—a straight-sided biscuit tin would do—against the float chamber adjust this until it is vertically parallel with the set-square. Then tighten the ring-clamp securely and the carburettor is bound to be in a vertical position.

It is not difficult to introduce the combined pipe and carburettor assembly to its proper place on the engine. Turn it on its side and pass it between the offside water hose and the radiator. Being rubber the water hoses either side can be slightly displaced. Remember that a smear of grease on the induction pipe flanges will make sure of an airtight joint. Apply this after removing the rag stuffing and just before repositioning the flanges.

Another method, without removing the induction pipe, is to chock the machine level on a hard surface and replace the carburettor as nearly as possible right. Check with a spirit level on the float chamber.

Reconnecting the Throttle Cable. There is an adjuster on the carburettor which pushes up the throttle casing, and this will probably need screwing down to get the pip on the end of the wire within the hollow brass plug for the set-screw to grip it. Tighten securely and reset the casing adjuster.

The Throttle Cable. There should be no perceptible play in this. To ensure this unscrew the casing adjuster a little at a time with the left hand while the right hand tests the backlash at the twist-grip, until play disappears. The smallest movement of the twist-grip should immediately open the throttle by the same amount.

The Twist-grip. This, like so many things on this unusual little cycle, is unorthodox. As the grip is twisted a small brass block within the grip is made to travel down a quick spiral. The wire is gripped in the block and instead of the winding action associated with the usual type of twist-grip the throttle wire receives a straight pull.

Releasing the dome nut and set-screw enables the pressure between the two sleeves to be altered. For those not familiar with the action of a twist-grip, turning it inwards, towards the rider, opens the throttle, while pushing it away from one, the natural movement, closes down. Best adjustment is when the grip just stays wherever it is turned, yet responds to the slightest push of the fingers to close it.

The Amal Monobloc Carburettor Type 363. Mark III models have this simpler instrument with its four external adjustments

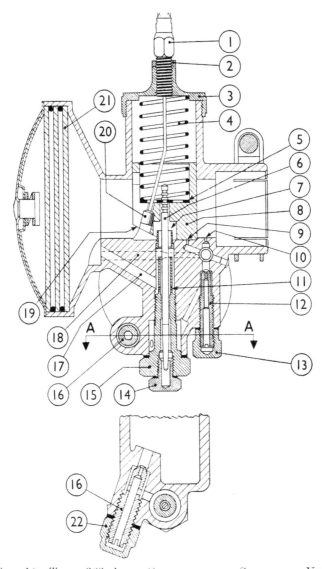

FIG. 18. TYPE 363 AMAL CARBURETTOR: SECTIONAL VIEW

1–2. Throttle cable adjuster and lock nut.
3. Knurled cap on mixing chamber.
4. Throttle return spring.
5. Jet needle clip.
6. Jet needle.
7. Primary air choke.
8. Throttle valve.
9. Pilot bypass.
10. Pilot outlet.
11. Needle-jet bleed holes.
12. Pilot jet.
13. Pilot jet cover nut.
14. Needle-jet plug screw.
15. Needle-jet.
16. Main jet.
17. Primary air passage.
18. Pilot air passage.
19. Throttle cutaway.
20. Cable nipple.
21. Air filter element.
22. Main jet cover nut.

(By courtesy of Amal Ltd. and Veloce Ltd.)

and "tickler." The filter/strangler enriches the mixture for starting. The pilot air-bleed screw, horizontal and next to the mounting stub, controls the petrol/air mixture for starting, idling and slow running. The throttle-stop screw is vertical and alongside the pilot screw and holds the throttle slightly open so that the engine will tick-over. The throttle valve cable control goes to the (right-hand) twist-grip on the handlebars and is the main control for the engine.

The correct settings for this carburettor as fitted to the LE Mark III are—

Main jet	65	Needle position	No. 3 (in middle groove)
Pilot jet	25	Throttle valve	No. 2

Cleaning Exhaust Pipe. To maintain the standard of performance clean out the silencer outlet pipe occasionally; a suitable time would be after decarbonizing the engine. A small wire brush or an old and flexible table-knife would be suitable.

6 Wheels and Brakes (LE and Valiant)

NEITHER wheel of the LE model is supported clear of the ground when the machine is on its stand, as has already been seen. The wheels, however, are very easy to remove and either can be raised clear of the floor without exerting strength, it being rather a matter of easily acquired knack. It is all done from the stand position, and by tipping and raising the cycle first on one side and then on the other.

When it is on its stand it can be tipped away from the operator without risk of overbalancing, until a block some 4 in. high can be slipped beneath the raised foot. If, then, it is allowed to come to rest and the performance is repeated at the other side, both feet of the stand will then be resting on 4-in. blocks. The machine is stable and the rear wheels is clear of the ground, convenient for cleaning, brake adjustment, or wheel removal.

From this stage it is quite simple to lift the front wheel. A wooden box or block about 8 in. high should be placed across the machine between the front mudguard and the radiator and resting on the ground. The operator now stands to the right of the front wheel, left hand on the twist-grip to steady the machine, right hand underneath the forepart of the front mudguard. A stout glove may be worn or a cloth pad carried on the palm. Lift the mudguard. The balance of the machine will permit the whole front of the cycle to be raised without effort. With the foot push the box or block underneath the radiator and below the engine cross-member. Let the mudguard down.

The front wheel should be raised to make cleaning easier or to enable the front brake to be adjusted. If it is a question of taking out the wheel to mend a puncture this can be done with the cycle on its stand. Removal of the wheel will bring both feet of the stand to the ground.

Removing the Front Brake Shoes. The best way of covering several points of front wheel maintenance will be to describe the removal of the brake shoes, for which it is assumed that the machine has been put on its stand without any additional blocking up. Tools wanted are a $\frac{7}{16}$ in. open-ended spanner (the spindle nut is somewhat masked and a ring spanner cannot be conveniently used), a $\frac{3}{16}$ in. open-ender for the pinch-bolt, a light hammer, and a punch or drift (or a 4 in. wire nail).

At the bottom of the near-side fork end a transverse $\frac{3}{16}$ in. pinch-bolt will be seen. This grips the spindle head and must be slackened, but need not be removed. Most of the remainder of the work is then done at the off-side fork. First slacken the brake adjuster and push it up so that the brake cable can be disconnected by slipping the brass end out of its socket in the brake lever. To do this it will be necessary to turn the slack in the cable so that it will pass through the slot on the outside of the lever.

Next, with the open-end $\frac{7}{16}$ in. spanner, remove the nut and lock-washer at the off-side end of the hub spindle. If the whole spindle turns, temporarily retighten the $\frac{3}{16}$ in. pinch-bolt. When the nut and washer are off slacken the pinch-bolt again. Now put the end of the drift, or 4 in. nail, into the small recess at the end of the spindle, and tap gently with the hammer to drive the spindle out of the off-side fork end. When it comes out of the fork the end will spring outwards, tension being factory-applied in this way to keep the forks in alignment. Leave the spindle in this position and go to the front of the machine.

Grasping the point of the front mudguard with the left hand, lift this slightly and with the right hand reach down and try to withdraw the spindle. It may be too stiff, in which case return to the off-side and tap it a bit farther. Try again from the front. There will come a point at which the spindle can be eased out with the hand. Put it down without letting go of the front mudguard and draw out the wheel forward. If the brake plate assembly drops out as the wheel comes away this is quite normal, but look out for the inner collar or distance piece which may fall and roll off somewhere.

The cycle will now settle forward on to both feet of the stand and the left hand can allow this to happen and be withdrawn from the front mudguard. It will be incidentally observed that the near-side fork end also "turns its toes out" which of course makes the spindle stiff to withdraw.

The Front Brake Shoes. Attention can now be given to the brake plate on which these are mounted, and which dropped away as the wheel was withdrawn. The shoes are now fully accessible and any reconditioning operations can be conducted at the bench.

When regular adjustment of the front brake has been taken beyond the point where the operating lever is at a right-angle, full braking power is lost. This is a dangerous state of affairs and to overcome it a pair of U-shaped steel pads, sold for a small sum by the Velocette dealer, should be fitted over the cam ends of the brake shoes. These will enable the remaining half of the linings' useful life to be used.

Examination of the brake shoes shows that at the ends bearing upon the flat cam connected to the brake lever the shoes end in a flat hard-steel plate. It is here that the pads are fitted. The other ends of the shoes are semicircular and bear upon a steel pin. No attempt should be made to fit the pads at this end.

Taking Out the Shoes. This can be done by protecting the hands with a stout pair of old gloves and then folding the shoes together as in closing a book. This is more easily done if the bolt and retaining washer are withdrawn from the semicircular or pivot end. As the shoes are grasped and folded together the link springs may fall out and they should be retrieved and set to one side.

Fitting the U-pads. The U-pads slip over the flat ends of the shoes. A little light tapping with the hammer may be needed to get them in place and to close the ends of the U-pads slightly so that they grip the shoes and cannot fall off again. Before replacing the shoes see that all the rivet heads are well below the surface of the linings. If any of them are lifting get them professionally clenched down. Should the condition of the linings be doubtful, or if there is grease or oil on them, abandon the idea of padding-up and get the dealer to exchange the shoes for relined ones. Take no risks with brakes.

Hook on the link springs points down and "fold" them back into position with the action of opening a book. Take the greatest care that the U-pads slip correctly under the large retaining washer riveted over the end of the brake cam. If the shoes seem unaccountably hard to get back verify that they have not been turned upside down. The metal is relieved at one side to clear the retaining washer just mentioned.

In refitting the pivot-pin bolt note that this must be located with the head on the inside—together with the washer under it—and the nut, with a smaller washer, on the outside of the brake plate. If the nut were on the inside and came adrift it would lock the wheel.

The brake cam requires no lubricant at the point where it operates on the shoes. A little oil may be sparingly applied to the lever bearing from the outside of the plate. Round the shoes and cam see that all grease and dirt are cleaned away.

When the wheel is reassembled it will be found that the cable adjuster starts again from the beginning of its travel. As the linings wear down and the lever comes again past the right-angle the shoes should be removed and exchanged at the dealer for a relined pair. One can buy and fit new linings and save a little money but riveting these on and chamfering off the leading edges is not a job for the amateur.

Wear Within the Drum. Before final reassembly the brake-drum surface, in the hub of the wheel, should be examined. It should be perfectly smooth and polished. If there are ridges or scores these should be skimmed down on a lathe as braking will be fierce and uneven. This is not to be expected, however, except after a considerable mileage.

The Brake Cable. Each time the adjustment of the shoes comes into question the front brake cable should be closely examined. If a single strand of wire is frayed scrap the cable at once. Do not wait until more strands part. Get a complete front cable assembly, inner and outer, from the dealer. It is false economy to try to fit a new length of cable within the old outer cover, and in any case the amateur is rarely able to sweat on nipples so securely to the cable ends that they will not rip out under heavy braking.

Reassembling the Wheel. Before beginning to put things back go over all bolts, nuts, washers, and threads with clean paraffin or petrol and a stiff bristle brush. Have everything spotlessly clean. It makes a great difference to ease of reassembly and subsequent dismantling. Much delay and hard work can be saved if all nuts are mated to their threads first so that they finger-tighten without effort. Wipe the spindle shank and thread with a trace of graphited grease.

Replace the brake plate in the wheel with the distance piece in position. Lift the front of the machine and introduce the wheel, slipping the torque-plate slot under the stud on the off-side fork member. Push the spindle through the near-side fork end and twist this slightly so that the spindle enters the hub. Work the spindle into position and pull the brake plate slightly aside to make visibly sure that the spindle passes through the distance piece. When the screwed end emerges at the off side twist the fork leg so that the spindle in turn enters the hole. The head of the spindle should sink slightly into the recess at the near side if it is correctly positioned. Put on the off-side washer and run the nut on a couple of threads.

Now go to the handlebars and firmly but not violently bounce the forks up and down once or twice to position everything correctly. Make sure that the torque plate has not come away from the stud in the off-side fork. Tighten the off-side spindle nut fully. Bounce the handlebars once again, then tighten the $\frac{3}{16}$ in. pinch-bolt.

Adjusting the Brake. Raise the front wheel clear of the ground by the block and box method previously described. Slip the front brake nipple into its housing on the lever. Spin the wheel, which should be perfectly free. Tighten the brake adjustment until it rubs very slightly, and lock the other nut on the adjuster. The slight rub will disappear in a mile or so as the brake pads settle down. It is best to make a point when on the road of using the front brake several times in the first mile or so.

The brake to start with may be squeaky and apparently ineffective. This is because the former faulty adjustment will have caused the linings to glaze. If the brake takes up noticeably on the hand control do not neglect to raise the wheel again and eliminate the slack. Always set brakes initially with a very slight rub. Persistent squeaks can be cured by lightly smoothing the glaze off the linings with fine sandpaper.

With new linings there is quite a rapid settlement calling for more than one take-up on the adjuster. The lining has to accommodate itself to the drum. Points to watch are that full braking power is obtained well before the lever comes up against the handlebar, and of course that the lower lever, on the drum plate, does not pass the right-angle.

Spoke Tension. Check the spokes whenever the front wheel is raised. Starting at the tyre valve, rotate the wheel slowly, tapping all spokes, first those at one side and then the other. If a spoke does not emit a clear note, but buzzes or rattles, it is loose. With a small adjustable spanner or a nipple key screw down the nipple protruding from the rim just enough to make the spoke ring true. On no account tighten any nipple more than this or the wheel will be pulled out of truth.

Broken spokes must be renewed at once. They nearly always snap at the hub end, the head breaking off usually because the spoke has loosened and been neglected. Unscrew the broken spoke and take it to the dealer as a guide to correct replacement, there being two lengths in the LE wheel.

It is impossible to fit a new spoke without taking off the tyre. As the new spoke may protrude far enough into the well of the rim to puncture the tube, the unwanted length must be clipped off so that the end of the spoke stays inside the nipple.

Removing the Rear Wheel. This can also be done with the machine on the stand. To get the wheel off the ground chocks can be put under the stand at each side, but for simple wheel removal there is no need to do this.

Front and rear spindles are the same size, but to take out the rear one a $\frac{7}{16}$ in. ring spanner can be used. The head of the spindle is at the off-side of the machine but there is no pinch-bolt, neither does the spindle have a lock-nut at the near-side end. Apply the ring spanner and turn till it is seen that no more of the shank is emerging. A punch can be lightly hammered against the spindle end, through the bevel casing at the near side, if it is difficult to remove. As it draws out, the distance-piece between the corner of the frame and the hub, like a metal cotton-reel, will probably drop away.

If the wheel feels loose it will now come away quite easily in the manner about to be described. If it is still apparently fast,

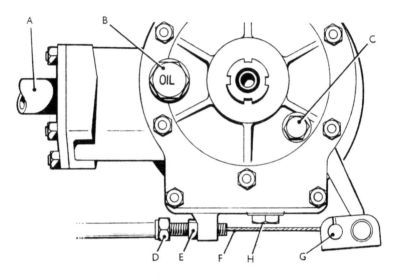

FIG. 19. BEVEL CASING, OIL FILLER, AND REAR
BRAKE ADJUSTER FOR LE AND VALIANT MODELS

A = Torque tube.	F = Brake cable.
B = Oil filler plug.	G = Cable nipple.
C = Oil level plug.	H = Oil drain plug.
D = Footbrake adjuster.	J = Brake lever.
E = Lock-nut.	

the brake will have to be slackened off to get the shoes clear of the drum but there is no need to disconnect the cable. With the brake slack an assistant is helpful for the actual wheel removal.

One person stands at the off side of the machine and lays it over at about 45°, but not more or petrol may spill from the tank. The right handlebar can be allowed to rest on the seat of an old chair or convenient box. The assistant then lifts the loose wheel at a point below the end of the rear mudguard. It has to be displaced sideways to part the internal gear within the brake-drum from the pinion on the inner face of the bevel casing. Once these two have disengaged the wheel can be drawn out below the mudguard.

The makers suggest that the machine should be laid completely over on its left or near side, the reverse of the above. If this is to be done the battery must first be removed—unless it is an unspillable type like the Varley Dry—and care also be taken about petrol spillage. Replacement, following the same drill in reverse, will be found somewhat easier than removal. The "cotton-reel" distance piece should not be overlooked.

The lock-washered nut on the near side of the bevel drive casing should not be tampered with either in removing or refitting the rear wheel. It looks as if it might be a lock-nut on the end of the spindle, but it is of course nothing of the kind. All that has to be removed is the spindle bolt and the distance piece.

The rear brake shoes are less easy to remove than those in the front hub because the brake back-plate in this case is integral with the inner face of the bevel drive housing. Taking off the offside pannier casing and tipping the machine over to the near side will considerably help in shoe removal. Otherwise the principle is the same as with the front brake, and U-pads can be fitted in a similar way. All the brake shoes on the LE model are interchangeable.

Brake adjustment also obeys the same rules. The arm operating the cam must not pass the right angle if maximum braking efficiency is to be retained. The brake pedal, between the nearside footboard and cylinder head, must fully apply the brake without touching down on the footboard.

Generally speaking the fitting of a rubber cover to the pedal is not to be recommended. Many people now wear rubber-soled shoes and when wet, even if the pedal rubber is well patterned, there is some risk of the foot slipping off. For the same reason if the metal serrations on the pedal wear smooth it would be wise to roughen them with a hacksaw blade.

Correct Use of the Brakes. Experienced riders try to avoid harsh brake application, especially in wet weather. When riding on treacherous surfaces change down through the gears as obstructions are encountered. Traffic lights are always better approached, when conditions are doubtful, in an indirect gear.

The Clutch Cable Adjuster. When excessive slack develops through clutch wear or stretching of the cable, adjustment can be made halfway along the cable at the extensible threaded sleeve (under the main frame member). Some play must be left.

7 The Viceroy Scooter

INTRODUCED in 1961, the Viceroy scooter is a 248 c.c. flat-twin two-stroke having a "square" engine (54 × 54 mm bore and stroke) transversely mounted forward. It drives by shaft to an assembly of clutch, four-speed gearbox and spiral bevel carried as a sprung unit with the rear wheel. Drive from clutch to gearbox is by enclosed duplex chain.

A heel-and-toe gear pedal is operated by the right foot, giving the effect of "one up and three down" selection but with all downward movements. On the left hand foot-board a pedal controls the rear brake, and forward of this is a foot switch for the 12-volt starter, electric car-type with silent engagement.

Hand Controls. These follow usual motor-cyle practice, with a lever-operated front brake and a twist-grip throttle for the right hand. The rider's left hand works the clutch lever, the horn button and dip-switch, and the flashing indicators.

There is an instrument panel with ammeter and speedometer, lighting and ignition switches, on the handlebars. As with the LE model the ignition switch has an Emergency position so that if there is battery trouble the machine can be walk-started.

The Amal Monobloc Carburettor. This is completely enclosed and there is no "flooding." To start the engine, pull out the fuel knob on the right of the front shielding, and the choke as well if the weather is cold. Switch the ignition to ON and firmly push the starter pedal. Do not run the engine too long with the choke closed.

To fill the tank, pull out the filler-measure cap below the instrument panel. Follow the maker's strict instructions: for two-stroke oil such as Shell 2T, put in three measures before each gallon of petrol (20 to 1, or five per cent). If self-mixing oil is used, add four measures before each gallon of petrol (16 to 1).

Half a gallon reserve of fuel is released when the fuel knob is both pulled out and twisted forward. The tank holds 2¼ gal.

Obtaining Neutral. Since there is no visible gear indicator, neutral position should be found by pushing down the heel pedal one to three times (this from top gear). After this a half-movement of the *toe* pedal will select neutral, as one can check by the free movement of the machine back or forth.

To push-start, engage second gear by one firm downward shift of the toe pedal (from neutral), hold out the clutch (left hand) and walk the machine forward, at the same time releasing the clutch and opening the throttle slightly. As soon as the engine fires, declutch and engage neutral (one down on the heel pedal followed by a half-stroke of the toe pedal). If the batteries are discharged, now switch quickly from Emergency to ON. With the batteries absent, the machine may still be ridden but not at more than 30 m.p.h.

At all times start from bottom gear (heel pedal). With a new machine the makers recommend maxima on the respective gears of 10, 16, 22 and 30 m.p.h. The fully run-in maximum in top is about 60 m.p.h. and normal fuel consumption will vary between 80 and 100 m.p.g. For hints about the use of the gears see page 56.

The Brakes. For normal stops, as when approaching traffic lights, close the throttle and let the machine lose speed. Then use both brakes gently together. It is always safer on wet or rough roads to slow by changing down, and to brake in a straight line.

Maintenance. Tyre Pressures. Check these weekly, or every 500 miles; both should be 18 lb, increasing the rear to 30 lb per sq. in. when a pillion passenger is carried (metric equivalents are 1·3 kg and 2·1 kg).

Top-up the batteries (under the dualseat) with distilled or clean rain water, keeping the level $\frac{1}{8}$ in. above the plates. Polythene batteries should be filled to the coloured line.

In the case of a new machine, drain the transmission at 500 miles—the drain plug is under the right-hand rear wheel valance and the machine should be hot from a run. Replace the plug, inject half a pint of neat petrol into the filler; replace this and run the machine gently for 2–3 minutes, engaging the gears. Then let the dirty petrol drain completely; finally refill to the level plug with $1\frac{1}{2}$ pts of SAE 50 gear oil. Repeat this process every 5,000 miles (8,000 km).

Occasionally apply a drop of light machine oil to all pivot points and exposed cable ends (clutch, brake, etc.). At 10,000 miles (16,000 km) the carburettor air-filter element should be removed, washed in neat petrol, dried and re-oiled.

The Clutch Control. As this settles down, after 500–1,000 miles, free movement of the lever (normally $\frac{1}{8}$–$\frac{1}{4}$ in.) may increase until the clutch does not free completely. There is a cable adjuster underneath the horn button plate, by the left handgrip. Release the locknut with a small adjustable spanner and adjust the longer nut until the correct free lever movement is regained. Remember to re-tighten the locknut.

Similarly with the brakes, also cable-controlled, the lever and pedal should fully apply the brakes before the end of the travel is reached. Adjustment for both brakes is the same, a ($\frac{1}{4}$) nut being turned right-handed until excess play disappears.

Carburettor Setting. This is correctly performed at the factory and no improvement will be made by altering it. The stop for the throttle and the pilot-air setting are pre-set; but the fuel filters may need attention at about half-yearly intervals. The nylon filter at the carburettor intake accumulates sediment;

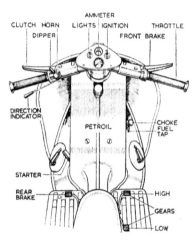

Fig. 20. Plan of Controls, Viceroy Scooter

carefully unscrew the brass nut above the union and lift it off without removing the pipe. Wash the filter in petrol, and use great care in reassembling the unit, to avoid leaks.

A second filter is fitted in the petrol tank, a long gauze. The tank has to be drained before it can be unscrewed. This filter is much less likely to need attention.

The Sparking Plugs. These can be reached by lifting the white grommets at the bottom of the legshields, incorporating the caps. Too much use of the choke, or sustained hard driving, may foul the KLG FE50 plugs and the points should be washed in petrol, brushing off with fine wire bristles. Set the gaps by bending the earth point of each to give a clearance of 0·025 in. For sustained hard driving fit a KLG FE 80, Champion N-3 or Lodge 2HLN.

Decarbonization. This may be desirable at 5,000 miles (8,000 km) if a loss of power is felt, especially on hills. Clearance of carbon from the exhaust ports will effect improvement; eventually the cylinder heads will have to be removed. Both are simple jobs, the ports and heads being quite accessible. Do not attempt to dismantle the carburettor, still less the steel reed-valve inlet block to which this is bolted.

The Contact-Breaker. After removal of the domed cover, clip-retained, in the lower front of the engine, the points can be examined. The correct gap is 0·15 in. It should not need re-setting more than annually. There is no maintenance for the generator (alternator) behind the stator plate and this should be left alone.

Changing Bulbs. Loosen the top screw on the headlamp and the light-unit reflector and glass lifts away. A three-wire lamp socket is bayoneted into the reflector and the main bulb is 24/24 W, 425. The pilot bulb, in a separate pull-out socket, is a 4 W, 222. The rear light combines stop and tail lamps in a twin 6/21 W; all bulbs are of course 12 V.

Wheel-changing. The car-type disc wheels are identical, but the front wheel dismounts at the spindle while at the rear the four hub nuts must be released. The front wheel forks have a large nut on the right side (seen from the saddle) and a pinch bolt on the left. After rolling the machine on its stand take off the large (spindle) nut, slacken the pinch-bolt, unscrew and finally withdraw the spindle.

With the wheel clear of the forks ease the brake-plate assembly out of the drum; leaving it attached to the cable. In refitting, finger-tighten the spindle and pinch nuts, bounce the wheel up and down in the forks once or twice to centre it, and re-tighten.

Before the rear wheel can be removed the silencer must be drawn out of the way. A rod passes lengthwise through this; locate it and release the rear (footboard) fastening of the rod. Loosen the front nut and draw the silencer to the rear until the wheel and its hub nuts are exposed.

8 The LE Mark III, Vogue, and Valiant Models

WITH the introduction of the LE Mark III, the Vogue and the Valiant, there are sporting and touring versions of the Velocette flat twins with the good performance provided by four-speed foot-change gearboxes. Let us first consider the LE Mark III as it affects the ordinary non-technical rider.

Four speeds are always better than three and a foot change is easier to operate than a hand control. The gear pedal, and the kick-start which replaces the hand lever, are both found close to the right foot in its natural position on the footboard. In a moment we shall see how much simpler and more positive both these controls are to work since at all times both hands can grasp the handlebars.

The Mark III: Other Features. Full-width aluminium hubs are fitted. There is a larger headlamp, faired into the handlebars, and the angle of these has a wider, more comfortable sweep than before. The lamp carries in its shell the ignition-lighting switch, the ammeter and the speedometer. The electric horn is sunk in the right legshield and an oil gauge can be fitted to the left shield. On the 12-volt model these arrangements differ from those on the police machine.

Further changes include the adoption of an Amal 363 monobloc carburettor (described and illustrated on pages 42–4). The controls work in the same way as with the earlier arrangement described on pages 3–5. The heavier crankshaft of the Valiant is fitted to the engine. It gives even smoother running than with the previous model and, by making higher revolutions possible, increases the power of the engine.

The Mark III machine can be started on or off its stand. One must first verify that the gearbox is in neutral. One then stands astride and, before switching on, gives two downward thrusts on the kick-start (this is really misnamed, since nothing so violent as a kick is needed). With the air control closed the rider pushes down the crank briskly, lifting his foot at the end of the travel. After repeating once more, he then switches on, and the next thrust of the foot should start the engine.

The Foot Change. This is much more convenient than the hand control. The rubber-covered "positive stop" gear pedal travels up or down through a narrow angle, returning automatically when the foot is removed. Each movement makes a gear change through a relay mechanism inside the gearbox. The change system follows current standard practice on most British motorcycles: "one up and three down." That is, to engage first gear one puts the toe of one's right foot *under* the pedal rubber, declutches, and lifts the pedal decisively as far as it will go. One

FIG. 21. THE VELOCETTE LE MARK III WITH DUALSEAT AND STREAMLINED PANNIERS

then releases the pedal and puts one's toe on *top* of the rubber ready for the change from first to second.

Second and Subsequent Upward Changes. The moment the machine is moving one closes the throttle, declutches again, and gives the pedal a smooth *downward* thrust, at once lifting the toe as the pedal stop is reached. Third and top follow in exactly the same way with ease and smoothness.

Changing Down. One moves the pedal *down* to change up, so one must move it *up* to change down. This is very much simpler to perform than to describe! One changes down, as with a hand change, on an open, or partly open, throttle. Easing rather than disengaging the clutch, one flicks the gear pedal lightly but firmly up with one's toe.

All these gear changes are fascinating in their silence and smoothness once one has acquired proficiency—as one very soon does. The rider can then use the gears far more, especially on slippery roads, when slowing down on the gears is safer than the most cautious use of the brakes.

Summarizing: the pedal moves *up* for bottom gear, *down* for second, third and top. In changing down the pedal movement is *up* in every case. Changes to a higher gear are made with a closed throttle, but changes to a lower gear always need the throttle partly open (the amount is not critical).

Finding Neutral. The drill for this is simplicity itself. One is, say, in top gear and has declutched after coming to a standstill. The clutch is kept out. Three successive upward movements of the gear pedal are followed by a single *light* downward tap, and neutral (which is halfway between first and second) will be found automatically. The clutch is then released. One should always come right down to bottom gear and then go halfway forward again, and not try to find neutral from second, as certain springs in the mechanism are designed only to be released when neutral is found from bottom gear.

Change Gear with the Toe. One should never try to lift the gear pedal with the heel. Riders with unusually large or small feet can adjust the angle of the pedal to make the toe fit more comfortably under it. If the pinch-bolt is slackened, the whole pedal can be slipped off the serrated shaft and replaced one serration up or down to give more or less room. Care should be taken that the pinch-bolt is properly retightened.

The foregoing gear-change drill applies to the Mark III LE model and also to the Valiant and the Vogue.

The Viceroy Scooter is similar but uses a heel-and-toe pedal.

THE VALIANT TWIN

This machine is in some ways a sporting version of the LE Mark III. Basically the same engine is used, but the Valiant is air-cooled and has push-rod-operated overhead valves, and each of the cylinders is fitted with an Amal 363 monobloc carburettor. Front hub and forks, gearbox, final shaft drive and rear hub are the same on both models. The AC–4 Miller generator, and 10 mm long-reach sparking plugs (*see* pages 19, 31) are also fitted.

The Valiant is of quite different appearance due to the use of a tubular cradle frame of ordinary "motor-cycle" pattern, the down tubes being twinned to accommodate the wide engine. Being air-cooled it has no radiator as on the LE, and instead of footboards the rider puts his feet on rubber-covered rests, as does the pillion passenger.

The petrol tank is mounted on the single top tube of the frame and holds more fuel than the "hidden" tank of the LE: three gallons instead of 1⅝. Engine, gearbox and rear drive all take the same amounts of oil as does the LE. Valiant rear suspension is by a proprietary make of enclosed oil-damped shock absorbers.

Engine Cowling. A neat system of enclosure gives the whole engine a very tidy appearance, and in the case of the "Veeline" model a separate frontal fairing enhances the effect. There is also a full-width handlebar screen on this model which, with legshields, protects the rider from the weather as completely as is possible with a motor-cycle.

Though it is primarily a sporting motor-cycle, many non-technical riders will find the lightweight Valiant much to their

FIG. 22. VELOCETTE VALIANT

taste but may wonder if the two carburettors make starting any more complicated. This in fact is not the case.

Starting the Valiant. After the petrol taps have both been turned on (the tank is constructed virtually in halves, each side feeding one instrument), Veloce Ltd. recommend that only the left-hand strangler, or air restrictor, should be closed. As with the Mark III LE (which uses a single Amal monobloc carburettor), the Valiant is best started with a fairly full throttle opening—a quarter to a third open. Before the ignition is switched on the starter pedal should be pushed down three or four times. Then the ignition switch is turned and a brisk thrust on the starter pedal should wake the engine immediately. Only in exceptionally cold weather may it become necessary to close the strangler of the right-hand carburettor as well.

When the engine is running the strangler is gradually opened. As soon as the engine is firing regularly the throttle can be closed down, but in cold conditions attempts should not be made to get the engine idling too soon. Better to leave it running briskly for a couple of minutes, for in any case an air-cooled engine warms up quite fast.

It is in the moments of starting from cold that most engine wear is caused, and the sump oil is diluted by unvaporized fuel seeping past the pistons. Warm up as quickly as possible—give it work to do, that is, get gently on the move, as soon as it will pull.

Decarbonizing and Valve Adjustment. In decarbonizing the Valiant engine there are a great many points of similarity to the LE model as mentioned on page 10 onwards. The Valiant, however, has the valve gear in the cylinder heads and with this type

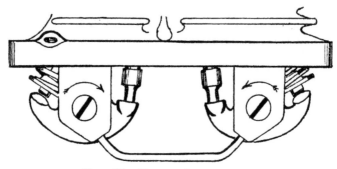

FIG. 23. VALVE ADJUSTMENT
(*See page* 63)

of engine it is highly desirable that the valves should be cleaned up and adjusted when the engine is freed from carbon.

Once again, as with the LE, it is far and away best to deal with each cylinder in turn and finish it. Detach the carburettor from one cylinder, the induction balance pipe, and the exhaust, and rocker oil feed pipes attached to the cylinder head. This latter job needs care because the hollow bolts are easily sheared or bruised, and the metal gaskets each side of the "banjos" may be lost or misfitted. The oil return pipe between the head and the sump also has to come away, after which the rocker cover, the polished component at the top of the cylinder head, can be taken off (it has one central—captive—retaining screw).

Getting the Valves Closed. Now take out the sparking plug from the *other* cylinder, the one on which work is not being done. Turn the engine slowly over on the kick-start and one will be able to feel the compression building up in the cylinder on which one is at work, which still has its sparking plug in position. Since there is compression both valves have closed, and as one can verify by feeling the rockers, clearance will be perceptible.

There are four cylinder-head nuts, between the second and third fins on the cylinder, and each should be unscrewed a little in turn until all four are quite free. Draw the head off the studs as far as the nuts will allow (it will come quite easily by finger strength), then run the nuts right off and put them carefully to one side in a tin lid, "patterned" so that each can be put back on its own stud.

The Push-rods and Tappets. As one draws the head off with one hand, separate the push-rods from the rocker tips with the other hand and press them in against the tappets. Have handy a stout rubber band (one cut from an old inner tube will do) and the moment the head is clear slip the band over the push-rods to keep them in place.

The point is *not* to remove the push-rods. If removed, the tappets will fall out of their guides and probably one will have to take the cylinder off to get them back. Try also to leave the gasket stuck undamaged to the cylinder face. It must go back the same way as it was fitted.

Cleaning the Piston Crown. The piston will be at the top of its stroke and the crown can be cleaned. Read the part of this book which deals with removing the carbon from the pistons and cylinder heads of the LE model, and observe the same precautions. Rub off as much carbon as possible with an oily rag, and scrape away hard deposits with a flat slip of hardwood or a stick of solder flattened to a chisel edge. Use engine oil as a softening medium. Polish the crown as much as possible but use no abrasive of any description.

Leave a little ring of carbon round the extreme edge of the piston to act as a seal. With the starter crank ease the clean piston slightly down the bore and wipe away all trace of carbon from the bore with a clean rag and a little engine oil. Paraffin can be used to wash all dirt from the cylinder head before the valves are removed.

The Head and the Valve Gear. Now take the cylinder head to the work bench. Have a tin lid in which components can be laid so that they will go back in the same places from which they came out. Unscrew both rocker pin locknuts and put them in the lid. Very gently tap, or push, the rocker pins out of the rockers. Each rocker pin carries a spring thrust washer above it and a hardened washer below. Pair them up in the proper positions.

Each valve spring has now to be compressed to get the cotters out. It is best to use a pair of spring-compressor tongs, though it can be done manually by the experienced. The cotters are exposed in halves and *must* be kept in these pairs. Once the cotter halves are out, the valve and spring will come away. There is a bottom washer round the valve guide—preserve it. One valve having been thus dismantled, deal with it and refit it before taking out the other one.

Cleaning and Grinding the Valves. Valve cleaning, grinding and polishing is discussed elsewhere in this book. If the inlet valve has a clean ring round its seat, leave this entirely alone but scrape off whatever carbon there is on the stem, afterwards polishing the stem lightly with smooth emery cloth. Carbon may cling obstinately to the valve head surface exposed to the combustion chamber and can be scraped or ground lightly off. The whole point is not to take a particle of metal off the valve or its seat more than can be avoided.

Oil the cleaned valve and try it in its guide before refitting. There should be no perceptible side play. Reassemble with the bottom washer first, then the spring, the collar; this assembly is then compressed and the cotter halves are stuck firmly in with a dab of grease.

Replacing the Rocker. Put back the rocker on its support, hardened steel thrust washer underneath and spring washer on top. These latter always go above the rockers—next to the arms that engage the push-rods. Set the rocker pins so that the tips bear as nearly as possible in the centre of the valve stems. This is because the eccentric movement causes the rockers to move eccentrically with the pins, and in one position they would strike the valve stems well out of centre. When set properly, lightly tighten the locknuts. The job will be finished when it is time to adjust the rocker clearances.

Before refitting the cylinder head have a final look to see that everything is impeccably clean. Before putting the head back take out the sparking plug as this will need a clean (*see* page 20), and if there is dirt in the orifice it will be blown out as the head is reintroduced. Check the gasket for position and general soundness—a damaged gasket will give trouble and should be replaced.

Re-positioning the Push-rods. Guide the push-rods through the apertures in the head, to engage with the rockers. Leave the rubber band in position until the last possible moment, cutting it if awkward to remove. Take the engine slowly round two complete revolutions to bring the piston once more to the top of the compression stroke, so that when the cylinder head nuts are tightened the valves will not be opened. Both cylinders come to top-dead-centre at the same moment, but while the one you are working on is at the top of the compression stroke with both valves closed, the opposite cylinder is at the top of the exhaust stroke with this valve open.

There is a great art in tightening the cylinder head nuts in "corner to corner" order, and each just a fraction at a time. Use the proper fitting spanner with unaided hand leverage. Over-tightening causes many troubles, not the least perhaps a fractured stud.

Setting the Clearances. Now it is time for the rocker clearances to be reset. Sizes needed: a 0·004 in. feeler gauge (blade) for the inlet, and a 0·006 in. for the exhaust: both unbruised. Slacken the previously lightly-tightened lock-nuts on the rocker spindles. Engage a screwdriver in the slotted head of the rocker spindle and slip the appropriate gauge between the rocker tip and the valve stem. Facing the job, turn the left-hand spindle clockwise, and the right-hand spindle anti-clockwise, to reduce the clearances. The gauge should slide through without jamming. Tighten the lock-nuts; re-check in case the spindles have moved during tightening (it is best to tighten up with the screwdriver pressed into the slot). Once the clearance is satisfactorily set, replace the cover. *See also* Fig. 23, page 60.

Deal with the opposite cylinder in exactly the same way. Clean and reset the sparking plugs. Finally, check that all oil pipes are in position. After a day's use go over the head nuts once more and tighten each the merest fraction again, as they settle down to some extent.

Adjusting the Carburettors. Though in general it is best to leave these alone, it is possible after decarbonizing that the idling may need readjustment. In this case deal with them one at a time. Remove one sparking plug, replace it in the suppressor cover, and wedge the plug body against the fins so that the plug can spark, to avoid an open circuit.

Start the engine and adjust the pilot-air screw until even running is obtained on the one cylinder. The screw may have to be as much as four turns open. Replace the sparking plug and remove the other one, wedging it in the same way. Repeat the pilot adjustment for the other cylinder.

Now refit the plug and start up on both cylinders. The engine will probably run too fast and the throttle-stop screws should be lowered a very small amount on alternate sides, keeping them in step. As the ignition timing does not retard immediately, do not close down the throttle-stop screws to the point where the engine stalls as the timing alters.

Whatever fine adjustments are made, they must be the same for each carburettor and should be altered by very small amounts alternately.

Veloce Ltd. emphasize that there is nothing to be gained under any normal conditions by changing jet or valve sizes. The only exception is very high altitude working, in which case the makers should be consulted. Standard sizes are—

Main jet	100
Pilot jet	15
Needle position	No. 3
Throttle valve	No. 2

An illustration of the Amal 363 carburettor will be found on page 43.

THE LE "VOGUE"

Introduced in the 1965 range, the LE Vogue is a highly developed *de luxe* version of the standard LE. Mechanically the variation is slight, and the Vogue is only some 20 lb heavier than the Mark III LE; the difference lies in the horizontally "lined" Mitchenall fibre-glass body with its light-coloured two-tone finishes.

A prolonged test of the fibre-glass shell was reported by *Motor Cycle* as showing no signs of deterioration after 11,000 miles. Minor damage to fibre-glass is easily repairable and the question of rust does not arise.

High-Output Alternator. The output of the electrical generator is 80 W, sufficient to balance the demands of the two 24/24 W headlamps which help to give the machine its bold and distinctive appearance. The Vogue is being marketed with 12 V equipment and a built-in starter, of the same type as that fitted to the LE and the Viceroy. Flashing direction indicators are an optional extra.

A larger petrol tank ($2\frac{1}{2}$ gal, 3 U.S., $11\frac{1}{3}$ litres) than that of the LE is fitted, with a reserve position giving a further six miles. Oil fillers, sparking plugs, cylinder heads and radiator cap are all accessible on lifting away the side panels. To release these, three "click" fasteners at either side are turned with the edge of a coin.

Instruments are not split up between the headlamp shell and legshield tops, as in the LE, but are neatly grouped in a panel forward of the handlebars. This arrangement is the same as that adopted for the Viceroy scooter.

For all overhaul and upkeep hints, Vogue owners should refer to the earlier pages of this book. Remarks relevant to the LE Mark III are valid for the Vogue.

THE VELOCETTE SINGLE-CYLINDER RANGE

Model	Capacity, Bore, Stroke, and Type of Engine	CR	Gear Ratios				Capacity Fuel	Capacity Oil	Susp F	Susp R	Size of Tyres Front in.	Size of Tyres Rear in.	Wt lb
Viper	349 c.c. 72 × 86 mm o.h.v.	8·5	5·5	6·6	8·7	12·6	3 g	½	T	PF	3·25 × 19	3·25 × 19	380
Viper Clubman	349 c.c. 72 × 86 mm o.h.v.	9·3	5·5	6·03	7·94	10·45	4½ g	½	T	PF	3·25 × 19	3·25 × 19	385
MSS	499 c.c. 86 × 86 mm o.h.v.	6·75	4·87	6·5	8·6	12·4	3 g	½	T	PF	3·25 × 19	3·25 × 19	385
Venom	499 c.c. 86 × 86 mm o.h.v.	8·0	4·87	5·87	7·7	11·2	3 g	½	T	PF	3·25 × 19	3·25 × 19	385
Venom Clubman	499 c.c. 86 × 86 mm o.h.v.	8·75	4·87	5·35	7·03	9·25	4½ g	½	T	PF	3·25 × 19	3·25 × 19	390
350 Scrambler	349 c.c. 72 × 86 mm o.h.v.	9·3	7·85	9·5	12·46	17·9	2¼ g	½	T	PF	3·00 × 21	4·00 × 19	335
500 Scrambler	499 c.c. 86 × 86 mm o.h.v.	8·75	7·25	8·58	11·41	16·65	2¼ g	½	T	PF	3·00 × 21	4·00 × 19	335
Endurance	499 c.c. 86 × 86 mm o.h.v.	8·0	4·87	5·87	7·7	11·2	2¼ g	½	T	PF	3·00 × 21	4·00 × 19	375
Viper Veeline	349 c.c. 72 × 86 mm o.h.v.	8·5	5·5	6·6	8·7	12·6	3 g	½	T	PF	3·25 × 19	3·25 × 19	398
Viper Clubman Veeline	349 c.c. 72 × 86 mm o.h.v.	9·3	5·5	6·03	7·94	10·45	4½ g	½	T	PF	3·25 × 19	3·25 × 19	403
Venom Veeline	499 c.c. 86 × 86 mm o.h.v.	8·0	4·87	5·87	7·7	11·2	3 g	½	T	PF	3·25 × 19	3·25 × 19	403
Venom Clubman Vee-line	499 c.c. 86 × 86 mm o.h.v.	8·75	4·87	5·35	7·03	9·25	4½ g	½	T	PF	3·25 × 19	3·25 × 19	408
Venom Thruxton 500	499 c.c. 86 × 86 mm o.h.v.	9 to 1	4·4 / 4·4	5·3 / 4·83	6·97 / 6·3	10·1 / 8·4	4½ g	½	T	PF	3·00 × 19R	3·50 × 19	375

Manufacturers: Veloce Ltd., York Road, Hall Green, Birmingham 28. *Extras:* Air filter, luggage grid, safety bar. For Clubman models—Rev-meter, light-alloy rims, megaphone exhaust.

Abbreviations. CR = compression ratio; F = front; R = rear; Wt = weight; T = telescopic fork; PF = pivoted fork; o.h.v. = overhead-valve.

(By courtesy of "Motor Cycle," London)

The Single-Cylinder Velocettes

9 The Various Models

MODEL GTP, a two-stroke, was produced from 1930 to 1938 (some export models were built in 1946). The engine is of the deflector piston type, 63 × 80 mm bore and stroke and capacity 249 c.c. An aluminium piston having a floating gudgeon-pin runs in a cast iron cylinder barrel. The cylinder head is of aluminium.

The foot-change gearbox has ratios 5·3, 7·1, 9·3 and 13·6 to 1. It is driven through a three-plate clutch by an oil-bath primary chain. A separate pump lubrication system is coupled to the throttle, and the tank holds $2\frac{1}{2}$ gallons of petrol and $3\frac{1}{2}$ pints of oil.

The K Series. These overhead camshaft four-strokes were first produced in 1925, and models KSS and KTS continued in the Velocette range until 1950. They are of 348 c.c., 74 × 81 mm bore and stroke, and the version known as the Mark II has an aluminium cylinder head.

Models MOV and MAC. The MOV was the first push-rod overhead valve machine produced by the company. It was marketed from 1933–48 as a 248 c.c. of 68 × 68.25 mm bore and stroke. The following year (1934) the series MAC was added, of 68 × 96 mm and capacity 349 c.c. It has been succeeded by the Viper models, also of 349 c.c. but 72 × 86 mm bore and stroke.

The MSS. This 495 c.c. machine was first made in 1935, of 81 × 96 mm bore and stroke. With the MOV it remained in production till 1949. The MSS was revived in 1954, and now has a light-alloy engine of 86 × 86 mm (499 c.c.). A sports version of the MSS is known as the Venom.

DETAILS OF THE MOV

This model has a single-port engine, forerunner of the "high cam-shaft" type. The timing-side pinion drives the oil pump and the timing cam wheel through an intermediate pinion. The short push-rods are worked through cup-ended enclosed rockers, totally enclosed and bearing on the cams. The overhead valve gear is positively lubricated and enclosed in aluminium cases.

The teeth on the timing pinions are cut and ground for long life and silence, and the cam spindles are extended on the outer side. Here an outrigger plate, bolted to lugs inside the timing case, gives additional support. The aluminium piston carries three rings, two compression and one scraper, and compression is 6·75 to 1.

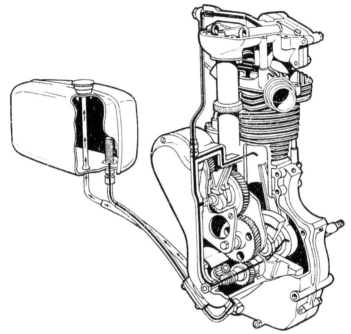

FIG. 24. THE MOV ENGINE: OIL CIRCULATION

Dry-sump lubrication is used, with a gear-driven pump and a half-gallon tank under the saddle. The flange-fitted magneto is gear-driven through a composition wheel.

Gearbox. Four speeds are fitted: 6·3, 8·4, 11·1, and 16·1 to 1. There is a right-hand pedal-operated change. This, as with many early Velocette models, gives "up for up," that is, upward gear changes are made by upward pedal movement. Post-war Velocettes have followed the now generally standard practice, "one up, three down," used by most British motor-cycle makers. However, with earlier models, the Velocette owner can choose the direction of movement he prefers, by fitting a new gear pedal, or in some cases by changing the cam plate. The operating mechanism is contained within the gearbox on all machines.

The MOV Frame. This is a brazed-joint affair with 1¾ in. top and bottom rails. There is 5 in. ground clearance and the lower part of the frame protects the crankcase. The single central-compression spring fork is adjustably damped, as is the steering.

Transmission Shock-absorber. This, with the primary chain, is oil-bath enclosed, the shock-absorber being on the engine shaft. The rear chain has the usual guard along its top run.

Brakes. These are of 6 in. diameter, with mud flanges, hand adjusters, and, within the front drum, the speedometer drive. Telescopic fork models have 7 in. front brakes, and spring-frame machines have 7 in. brakes back and front.

The silencer is of the characteristic flattened pattern, with built-in fishtail, retained for many years on the majority of Velocette models. Exhaust pipe and silencer are chromium-plated.

Lighting and Ignition. A 6-volt dynamo is driven by belt from the engine shaft and charges a 13 amp-hr accumulator. The head-lamp uses 3-watt and 24-watt bulbs, and switch and ammeter are as usual carried in the shell. The magneto, as already mentioned, is gear-driven from the timing.

A detachable rear-half back mudguard gives access to the wheel, and there are prop, front and rear stands. Tyres are 3·25 × 19 in. Other dimensions are: weight, 275 lb, wheelbase 52¼ in., height 27½ in. Maximum speeds are 60–65 m.p.h.

MAC AND VIPER

The MAC resembles the MOV apart from such points as larger engine size (348 c.c.), higher compression (6·75 to 1), gear ratios (5·5, 7·3, 9·6, 14), weight (280 lb) and maximum speed (up to 70 m.p.h.). These details refer to models up to 1939. After 1950 the MAC has an all-alloy engine, telescopic forks, and adjustable rear suspension of the pivoted-fork variety. Weight of the MAC has increased to 355 lb (161 kg).

The Viper is a 349 c.c. sports model of similar general characteristics to the Venom (and MSS). Though the engine volume of the Viper is the same as that of the MAC, its bore and stroke are 72 × 86 mm and it weighs 370 lb (168 kg).

THE EARLY MSS

This in general specification always closely resembled the MAC. With a compression plate the ratio is 6 to 1, without it 6·4 to 1. Solo gears are 4·4, 5·3, 6·9, and 10·1. Petrol capacity is 3½ gal, brakes are 7 in., and tyres 3·50 in. section front and 4 in. rear, on 19 in. rims. Wheelbase is 55 in., clearance 4¾ in., and weight 335 lb. Speeds are up to 75 m.p.h. solo, 60 m.p.h. with sports sidecar. It is interesting to compare these dimensions with those of the Venom and MSS, which have gear ratios of 4·97, 5·91, 7·78, and 11·24, tyres of 3·25 × 19 in., weight 375 lb, and the 86 × 86 mm, 499 c.c. engine.*

Elsewhere in this book (pages 65, 121) the Venom Thruxton 500 road racing machine is described. As the name indicates it is a development of the 499 c.c. Venom with higher gears (TT close ratios optional) and greater power output.

THE KSS (AND KTS) MODEL

This was the outcome of high-speed reliability work experience. It has a single-port bevel-drive overhead-camshaft engine. The massive flywheel assembly has a roller bearing on the driving side and a double-row ball bearing on the timing side. The steel connecting-rod has a single-row roller bearing big-end and a little-end bush for the fully-floating gudgeon-pin. The domed piston is recessed to clear the valves and has three rings—two compression and one scraper.

The cylinder head and rocker box form a single casting in aluminium alloy with inserted valve seats. With compression plate the ratio is 6·2 to 1, without it 6·8 to 1. Valve and rocker gear is totally enclosed and positively lubricated. Eccentrically mounted rocker spindles provide tappet adjustment. A double-acting pump takes oil from the half-gallon saddle tank to the bearings and returns excess to the tank.

FIG. 25. O.H.C. TAPPET ADJUSTER (KSS AND KTS)

Clutch and Gearbox Frame. The clutch has seven plates and the inserts are fabric. With a 17-tooth gearbox sprocket ratios of 5·6, 6·8, 9, and 13 to 1 are provided. The cradle frame is brazed.

Chains. Primary is of ½ × 0·305 in. running in an oil bath. Secondary is of ⅝ in. pitch.

* *There are several sets of gear ratios available for the Venom and MSS models.*

Other Dimensions. Wheels of 19 in. have a 3·25 in. front and 3·50 in. rear tyre, with 7 in. brakes. The rear brake, sprocket, and chain remain in position when the rear wheel is detached with its two self-contained journal bearings. Ground clearance is 4½ in., height to saddle-top 28 in., wheelbase 55 in. and unladen weight 333 lb. Maximum speed is 75 m.p.h.

MODEL KSS

This has sports mudguards and a smaller section front tyre. Otherwise the specification follows that of the KTS.

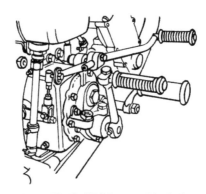

FIG. 26. THE KSS, KTS AND MSS ADJUSTABLE
FOOT CHANGE

(*By courtesy of "Motor Cycle"*)

Valve Timing—KSS (Mark II) 1936–9: Cam K 17/7

Inlet opens	. .	35° before top dead centre
Inlet closes	. .	65° after bottom dead centre
Exhaust opens	.	70° before bottom dead centre
Exhaust closes	.	30° after top dead centre

KSS 1947–50: Cam K 17/10

Inlet opens	. .	34° before top dead centre
Inlet closes	. .	47° after bottom dead centre
Exhaust opens	.	64° before bottom dead centre
Exhaust closes	.	29° after top dead centre

In each case timing is set with 0·025 in. clearance on both valves, running clearances being 0·006 in. inlet and 0·01 in. exhaust (*see* page 84).

10 Control and Lubrication of the "Singles"

CHECK oil levels before taking the machine on the road. Oil tanks should be filled to 1½ in. of the top. Remove both plugs from the gearbox and pour in engine oil slowly until it drips from the level plug orifice. Never use gear oil or grease.

Starting. Make sure that the gears are in neutral. Turn on the petrol tap (under the tank). Flood the carburettor slightly by depressing the float chamber button until petrol is just seen to ooze from the top of the float chamber. Excessive flooding not only wastes petrol but makes the mixture too rich and starting may then be difficult or impossible. If the weather is cold close the air lever on the carburettor. If the model has hand ignition control give it about half advance.

Get astride and lift the exhaust valve by the trigger on the left handlebar. Turn the engine slowly over once and allow the kick-start to rise. Depress it once more, and just before the crank reaches the bottom of the stroke release the exhaust lifter. The engine should start at once but if not it is probable that the exhaust lifter has been released a little too late. Some riders prefer to start on full compression after one turn with the exhaust valve lifted. In this case beware of a backfire.

As soon as the engine fires open the throttle a little to make it run briskly, to get the oil circulating and warm up quickly. After a few seconds one should be able to open the air control and move the magneto lever to about three-quarter advance.

Engaging the Gears. Throttle down so that bottom gear can be engaged without clashing. If the clutch is sticky pull up the lever two or three times, periodically "trying" bottom gear until it will engage without noise. It may be necessary to rock the machine back and forth a little. Move away with a small throttle opening, and as soon as the machine is on its balance make a decisive full movement of the pedal to engage second gear. This can be done very quickly with the throttle closed and no more than a "tip" of the clutch. Engage third gear at 15–20 m.p.h. Always make a full movement of the pedal. Do not rush to get into top. In traffic or on wet or slippery roads a powerful motor-cycle is always more controllable in third, or under bad conditions, second gear.

Many motor-cyclists have the slovenly and dangerous habit of making upward movements of the gear pedal by hooking the foot over it and pulling up with the back of the heel. Adjust the pedal so that the toe can be slipped under it instantly and easily. The pedal should be set down somewhat from the horizontal so that all movements of it come naturally with the foot swivelling upon the rest.

The clutch, too, should never be used save for changing gear, starting away, and stopping. At all times when the machine is at rest come quickly down through the gears into first, and from this position slip into neutral. If one finds neutral from second this leaves the centralizing spring partly in tension.

Riding Position. With handlebars and footrests widely adjustable, the best possible riding position should be secured in the interests of comfort and safety. Clutch and brake levers are easier to grasp quickly if brought up towards the horizontal so that the fingers fall naturally upon them instead of the rider having to extend the arms to reach round the handgrips.

Engine Lubrication. Three types of lubrication system are in use on the single-cylinder models. Starting with that on the two-stroke GTP model, throttle and oil supply are here interconnected so that the engine receives oil proportionate to the load. If the carburettor is removed or the engine dismantled the pump should be readjusted so that the control sleeve is at its lowest position when the throttle is shut.

If the engine receives an excessive amount of oil at low speeds pull out the split pin from the pump adjusting screw to allow this to be turned in the sleeve. As a slight movement of the screw has a considerable effect on the pump not more than a quarter of a turn of the screw should be made at once. The supply is cut down when the screw is turned clockwise. When finally a correct setting has been achieved, insert a new split pin and open out the ends.

Summer and Winter Oils. On all models Veloce Ltd. recommend a change of normal grade oil when the air temperature exceeds, or falls below, 60°F (15°C). Higher temperatures call for an increase of one grade—to 40 SAE—while below 60°F a 30 SAE oil should be used. Multigrade oils of the approved makes can, however, be used in the same ranges winter and summer. Additives are unnecessary and should not be mixed with the approved oils.

Overhead Camshaft Models. Lubrication here gives a gravity supply to the feed side of the double gear pump. The pump is driven by a coupling off the magneto spindle. Oil is forced through a recess in the pump cover into the timing case and pressure is built up which sends the oil, via the vertical shaft cover, to the top bevel housing. To prevent foreign matter choking the jet the

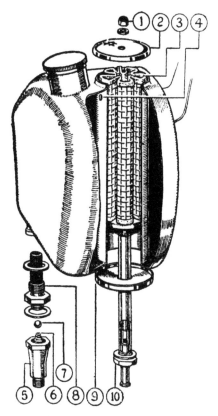

Fig. 27. Oil Tank, Ball Valve and Filter (Most Models)

1. Oil tank filter stud nut.
2. Oil tank filter cap—top.
3. Oil filter element—replace every 10,000 miles.
4. Outlet to tank.
5. Ball valve body.
6. Ball valve spring.
7. Ball valve ball.
8. Oil strainer assembly.
9. Oil tank filter cap—bottom.
10. Oil tank filter tube assembly (remove and clean in petrol each 2,000 miles).

hollow shaft connecting the oil pipe to the bevel housing has four small holes each the same size as the jet.

A spring-loaded ball valve is fitted in the timing side mainshaft: a ball seating on the inside of the left-hand-threaded nut is screwed to the end of the shaft. The works setting allows the ball to lift at a pressure of 10 lb per sq in. Constant pressure is maintained on the big-end by the oil forced through the mainshaft and an oilway in the flywheel registering with another drilled in the crankpin. Oil is thus sent direct to the centre of the roller track, surplus being thrown off to lubricate piston and cylinder bore. Excess drains into the sump to be picked up by the scavenge side of the pump and returned to the tank.

Surplus oil in the cam chamber lubricates the valve stems and guides by the movement of the camshaft, excess finding its way to the sump via the return pipe on the driving side of the engine. To vary the oil supply, the adjusting screw is turned clockwise to increase the flow and, of course, anticlockwise to decrease it. Adjustment should be made with the engine warm and by not more than a quarter-turn at a time. To check the adjustment remove the tank cap and observe the return flow, which should be practically continuous when the oil is warm.

An additional check can be made with an oil gauge, which should be screwed into the hollow bolt connecting the oil pipe to the bevel housing. This hole is normally blocked by a plug. A gauge pressure of 9–10 lb will indicate that the top bevels are well supplied with lubricant. Pressure up the vertical shaft without a steady return to the tank is insufficient, and in this case the adjusting screw must be turned clockwise until the oil flows freely. Conversely, a steady return to the tank without pressure in the shaft is useless, and attention to the ball valve in the timing side mainshaft is required for both troubles.

Pressure without return suggests a ball valve restricted due to a stretched or too strong spring, the remedy being replacement. Return without pressure suggests a ball stuck open due to a weak spring. Again a new spring should be fitted. To be sure that the ball seats perfectly in the nut it can be given a tap with a soft metal punch and a light hammer. Excessive smoke at starting may be due to the crankcase ball valve sticking open. Rectify by dismantling, cleaning and reseating the ball.

Draining Oil and Cleaning Filters. Drain the oil and refill with new lubricant at least every 1,000 miles. Oil in a new machine should be discarded at 500 miles and renewed. Every 2,000 miles remove the filter in the oil feed union at the bottom of the tank and thoroughly clean it in petrol, letting it dry before replacement. The tank itself should be similarly cleaned out.

Fabric Oil Filter. The filter element shown in Fig. 27 should be renewed every 10,000 miles or less and the old one discarded. It is not necessary to remove the tank to do this, though removal makes the tank easier to wash out. Regular renewal of this filter and cleansing of those in the feed union and crankcase enables oil changing to be postponed to 1,500–2,000 miles.

The four small holes in the hollow bolt at the top bevel housing, and the oil jet, should be removed at the same time and cleaned in petrol. Replace the fibre washers if they show signs of wear. To clear the engine of its residue of old oil start up with the return pipe to the tank disconnected and discharging into a tin. When clean oil issues from the pipe reconnect it.

Detergent Oils. Many modern lubricants are treated with detergent additives which will remove all internal dirt from the engine surfaces. For this reason it is well not to use such oils in an engine known or suspected to be internally dirty. The suspended matter can choke the oilways and cause lubrication failure. When an engine has been stripped and thoroughly cleaned internally the subsequent use of a detergent oil will maintain it in sludge-free condition.

Gearbox Lubrication. With a new machine the gearbox should be drained and refilled at 500 miles as with the engine. Subsequent draining and refilling of the gearbox at each 1,000 miles will be sufficient. Engine oil, not gear oil or grease, must be used in the box and the correct level maintained—checked when the machine is standing level as well.

Wheel Bearings. These on the larger models are intended to be repacked with grease at each 10,000 miles, no attention being given otherwise. Retaining washers inside each bearing prevent grease leaking into the hub centre, which should not be filled with grease. Though some models have hub greasers, it is better not to use these but to repack at regular mileages. Indiscriminate use of a grease gun can result in surplus finding its way on to the brake linings. At least they will be rendered useless and at worst a serious accident may be caused through brake failure at a critical moment. Grease-fouled linings cannot be cleaned and must be renewed.

Chain Lubrication. The primary chain, enclosed in an oil bath, requires no attention apart from periodical replenishment through the inspection hole in the front of the case. The case holds about a quarter-pint and should not be overfilled. The rear chain should be lubricated at regular intervals with an oil can. At 1,000–1,500 miles take it off, soak it in paraffin and when clean hang it up to dry. It can then be placed in a tin of warm graphite grease which will penetrate the rollers. Some riders swear by "cooking" the chain in melted tallow.

11 Decarbonizing

CARBON deposit is a combination of fuel soot, road grit, and burnt lubricating oil. Its removal from a new engine is desirable at 2,000–3,000 miles. Afterwards, the engine, particularly a four-stroke, can run for much greater mileages without attention. When carbon accumulates appreciably it causes falling-off in power, especially on hills, and the exhaust note loses its hardness, becoming flat or muffled. Detonation or pinking is also more frequent, happening not only during hill-climbing and pulling under load but also as an accompaniment to acceleration.

Preparing to Decarbonize. To get the machine ready raise it on the back stand. With a tin of paraffin and a bristled brush clean the whole exterior of the engine. Take out the tools and verify that the correct spanners are present. Have one or two boxes or tins to receive components, especially those liable to loss.

All parts impeding access to the cylinder must first be removed. In most cases this calls for detachment of petrol pipe, carburettor, exhaust pipe, and sparking plug. Then the four bolts holding the cylinder head are removed and the head is lifted off. Next the engine is turned over so that the piston is at bottom-dead-centre, after which the four nuts retaining the cylinder are detached.

(Do not unnecessarily remove the cylinder barrel from a four-stroke. The piston may become disturbed and the engine may develop heavy oil consumption.)

In lifting the cylinder considerable care is necessary to prevent the piston falling out and banging against the crankcase mouth. This will be avoided if a hand is passed beneath the cylinder as it is lifted and the piston is supported. Once the cylinder is removed the crankcase mouth should be covered with a cloth.

Spring circlips retain the floating gudgeon-pin and one of these must be removed. There is a slot beneath the Velocette gudgeon-pin circlip by which one side of one circlip can be lifted free with the tang of a file. Leave the other circlip untouched. Before finally removing the piston note which way round it is fitted and with a pointed steel marker scratch a capital "F" inside the front of the skirt if this has not been done already. It is just as important to replace a four-stroke piston the same way round since the rubbing surfaces become mated.

Removing Piston Rings. On two-stroke models it is desirable to slip off the piston rings at each decarbonizing to make sure they maintain compression at optimum. Use a ring tool or three pieces of tin about ¼ in. wide slipped under the rings in turn and spaced out. Rings in a two-stroke are prone to stick in the grooves since they cannot rotate and have no self-clearing tendency. Gummy

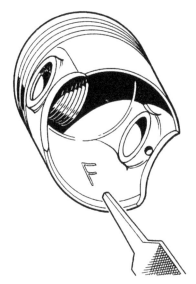

FIG. 28. MARKING THE INSIDE OF THE PISTON

oil can be removed with paraffin, and carbon behind the rings should be cleared with a chip of hardwood so as not to scratch the groove.

The rings should be quite bright all round. Any dull patches will indicate that they are not bearing properly and it is best to renew them, as also if there is up and down play in the grooves. Where it is necessary to fit new rings to a four-stroke they should be checked for clearance by inserting them in the cylinder barrel about an inch up the bore. Push them up one at a time with the ringless piston to ensure that they are level. Insert a 0·010 in. feeler gauge in the gap between the ends of each ring, which is the correct clearance. Should the gap close when the ring is pushed in, the size is unsuitable. Although the gap can be reduced with a file this is not an easy job for the amateur.

Push-rod Overhead-valve Models. In these the saddle should be lifted by loosening the front bolt, and the petrol tank removed

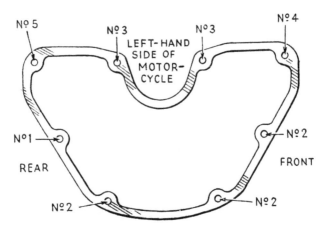

FIG. 29. LOCATION OF MAC ROCKER COVER BOLTS

No. 1 is the longest bolt. The others are identified numerically in decreasing length.

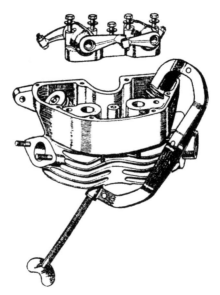

FIG. 30. THE CYLINDER HEAD AND ROCKER ASSEMBLY (MAC MODELS)

Rocker bearing bracket assembly removed. All five bolts are shown withdrawn, but only the two end ones and the centre one need be removed, and the other two which hold the bearing caps should be held tight. The compressor KA163/2 is shown in use.

after the front and rear fixing bolts have been removed. The petrol pipe must be disconnected after both taps have been turned off. Take out the sparking plug. Unscrew the knurled ring on top of the carburettor mixing chamber and withdraw the slide. Loosen the clip holding the exhaust pipe to the cylinder head and remove the pipe.

Next to be unfastened are the bolts holding together the sides of the rocker-box and the covers, then the nuts holding the top flange of the push-rod tube. By taking off the three bolts holding the rocker-box to the cylinder head, and by loosening the gland nut on the push-rod tube, the rocker-box can be lifted away.

Four holding-down nuts secure the head. Between head and barrel there is a copper washer which should be preserved. Four long studs retain the barrel to the crankcase, and one must be careful to prevent the piston falling out and striking the crankcase.

Grinding the Valves. Valves and seats generally require some attention. Grinding paste is sold in coarse and fine grades, and the fine alone should be used. A tool to grip the valve stem or a

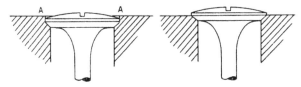

Fig. 31. Valve Seat Pocketed (left a–a)
Right—Further Grinding will soon Pocket this Valve.

suction cup to hold the head will be required. Smear a little thoroughly mixed paste round the seat and oscillate briskly backwards and forwards until the paste ceases to cut and the valve resonates or "sings." Lift, redistribute the paste, and resume, turning the valve slightly. Never rotate continuously. Proceed only as far as is necessary to produce a fine continuous seating or line right round. When satisfied, wash off valve and seatings in petrol to get rid of all traces of grinding paste.

Badly pitted seats are best dealt with by a cutter which will skim a trifle of metal off both seats, thus also preventing the valve becoming pocketed. The valve should rest on the surface of the head and if it sinks into it the gas flow is obstructed. Valve seats on most Velocette singles cannot be refaced by a cutter and a 45° stone must be used.

Refitting the Rocker Box. If not pulled down evenly upon the head the rocker box may be distorted. Considerable care should be taken that both push-rods are properly located and engaged with the rocker cups. Rocker-box and valve cover faces should be cleaned down to the metal and coated with jointing compound before they are re-mated. Tighten all nuts gradually and evenly and verify several times that everything is lining up correctly. If

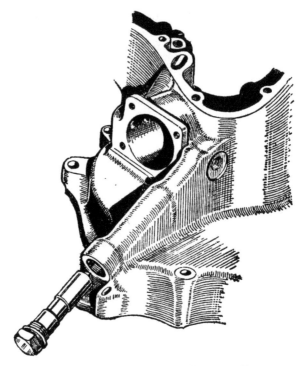

FIG. 32. THE CRANKCASE SUCTION FILTER

a component becomes bent or distorted it may be very difficult to put right.

General Hints on Carbon Removal. If the cylinder head is of cast iron an old screwdriver or blunt knife can be used to scrape away the carbon. It may also be soaked off by immersing the head overnight in caustic soda solution (one pound added slowly to a gallon of water). The solution acts more quickly if heated, and in a few minutes if boiling hot. Hot or cold it should not come in contact with the skin and the hands should be quickly rinsed in warm water if this happens.

Suspend the head in the solution with a wire through a port for easier removal. When cleaned it should be thoroughly washed in clean water to get rid of all caustic, and dried quickly or it will rust. A rust inhibitor can be usefully applied to the outer surfaces.

Light Alloy Heads and Parts. These must on no account be touched with caustic, which will destroy them, nor scraped with

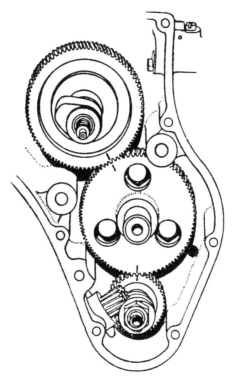

Fig. 33. Positions of Timing Marks (MAC, MSS Models)
The intermediate gear spindle bolt heads are also visible
through the holes in the gear.

iron tools as scratches are unavoidable. Use instead a heavy stick of tinman's solder beaten flat and trimmed off like a chisel, or an oak stick with a chisel edge cut at one end. To remove carbon from the inner surfaces of an alloy head a fine wire brush can be cautiously used. Wetting with paraffin aids carbon removal.

Metal polish will give a mirror finish to the piston crown and this delays further carbon formation. Wash away all traces of polish with petrol. Emery cloth can be used on iron parts but not on alloy as the particles become embedded in the soft metal.

Power-driven buffing tools, if available, are of course, far and away best to use on iron or alloy.

Reassembling the Engine. The piston having been already marked as suggested earlier, there will be no trouble about re-fitting it the right way round. Irrespective of type, every piston should be refitted to its cylinder the same way round as before.

If a metal to metal joint is used between head and cylinder this should be examined before reassembly for signs of burned oil which will indicate blowing. The joint may require regrinding using the fine valve paste. Afterwards, wash thoroughly with petrol. The thinnest possible coating of grease will help the surfaces to form a gas-tight joint and it is important to tighten the holding nuts evenly a fraction at a time. Work diagonally from one to another.

Overhead-camshaft Models : Removal of Cylinder Head. Pro-cedure as in decarbonizing is followed, beginning with detachment of the petrol tank. This is held by two front and one rear bolts. The rubber buffers are of different sizes and should not be mixed up. Take out the carburettor slide, uncouple the exhaust pipe and disconnect the exhaust valve lifter (on the head). Take away the Y-shaped oil drain pipe.

The vertical camshaft drive cover is secured by gland nuts at bottom and top, and after loosening, these should be moved well clear of the threads. Just above the bottom-bevel bush-housing there is a spring jump ring in a groove in the cover. It should be prised out and slid up the outside of the cover. Now the cover can be moved down into the bottom-bevel bush-housing, exposing the top coupling.

The housing cover of the top bevel is secured by four nuts and should be taken off. Now rotate the engine until the marks on the top bevels are in register, which may take up to 21 turns depending on the piston position when the engine stopped. The slot or mark at the top of the vertical shaft will be in line with the crankshaft, and the piston will be at the top of the compression stroke, when the bevel marks are lined up. The cylinder head can then be removed by unscrewing the holding-down bolts. A special box spanner is provided by the makers.

Valve Removal. Loosen the locknuts on the rocker pins and remove the valve covers. Using a valve spring compressor bearing at one end on the top washer and at the other on the centre of the valve head, compress the spring and lift out the cotter parts. The valve will come away as the compressor is released. The springs, with their top and bottom washers, cannot be taken out until the

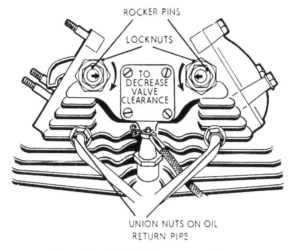

FIG. 34. O.H.C. CYLINDER HEAD

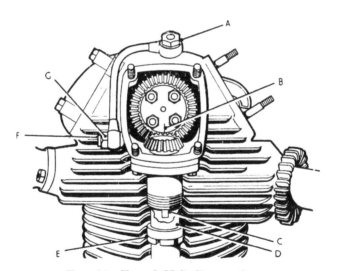

FIG. 35. THE O.H.C. BEVEL GEAR

A = Oil union.
B = Timing mark register.
C = Correct position of coupling.
D = Shaft casing.

E = Gland nut.
F = Plug for attaching oil gauge.
G = Hollow bolt securing oil pipe.

Piston at T.D.C. of compression stroke when couplings are as shown.

rockers are away, and for this the springs must be recompressed. First, however, a washer, supplied with the tool, is placed over the tip of the decompressor screw, both to provide a bearing and to prevent damage to the valve guide, against which the screw now presses.

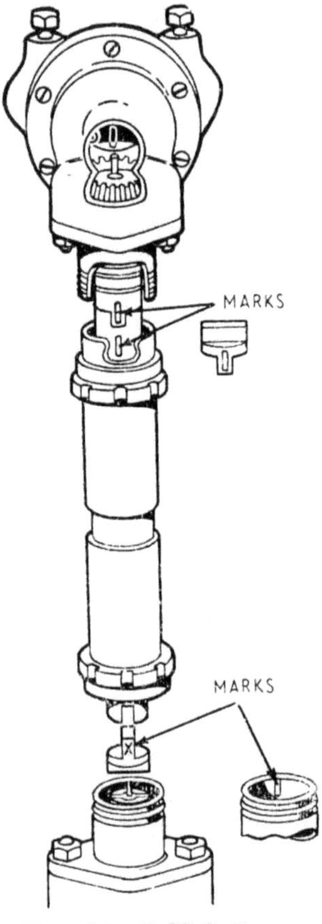

As the spring is compressed again the rocker is brought clear enough for the pins to be unscrewed, after which, pins, rocker and thrust washer can be removed. Next, of course, the spring will come away with top and bottom washers as mentioned.

Rebuilding the Valves and Adjusting the Tappets. The valves are cleaned and ground as necessary (*see* page 79). Then first insert the bottom washer of one spring, the spring, and the top washer; and compress. If the rocker bush is clean replace the rocker. Clean the shaft, oil the bearing surface, and refit, bearing in mind that the thrust washer must be fitted between the rocker left-hand side and the threaded end of the pin. Screw in the rocker spindle as far as it will go without using undue force.

Now screw back the spindle until the arrowhead marked on the end, inside the hollow of the hexagon, is horizontal and pointing inwards, that is, the arrows will be pointing at each other. With the rocker fitted the valve spring can be released. The valve, with stem clean and oiled, is inserted normally through the guide, the top washer being man-oeuvred as necessary for the stem to pass through. When the valve head is seated, compress the spring and refit the cotters, which should fully engage the serrations on the stem. Release the spring and the clearance may be reset.

MARKS

MARKS

Fig. 36. O.H.C. Drive

Before adjusting the rocker pins make sure that the camshaft has not moved and that the bevel marks are still in register. Clearances are 0·006 in. inlet and 0·01 in. exhaust. The rocker spindles are turned to move the arrows down to decrease and up to increase the clearances, which should be set cold. Feeler blades should be used. Once correct clearance has been gained screw the locknut up tightly.

Camshaft Dismantling. Camshaft and top bevel gears should not be taken apart unless the rider is skilful. By removing the two nuts securing the bevel gear bush-housing to the top bevel assembly this, together with the bevel pinion, can be pulled out. It is important to note the number of paper packings present as a similar number must be replaced (using the correct thickness as supplied by the makers).

The camshaft is removed by releasing the four screws retaining the cover at the sparking-plug side of the cylinder head. Again the number of packing shims between cover and head must be noted as these fix the lateral position of the camshaft. Next the nuts securing the bevel housing flange to the cylinder head are unfastened, and the housing, complete with camshaft bevel wheel and cam, can then be withdrawn.

Should it be necessary to separate the cam from the shaft a special puller is required, since the camshaft housing will be damaged if the shaft is pressed out of the cam. This is fitted to a part of the shaft larger in diameter than the parallel part taking its bearing in the bevel housing. Thus it is necessary to expand the bearing before the shaft can be freed, and this is done by immersing the housing in boiling water. The aluminium then expands and allows the shaft to come clear. A key locates the cam and must be moved.

Refitting the Cylinder Head. Any sign of blowing at the joint faces means that a new gasket must be fitted. The valve spring covers should be put back with new paper gaskets and jointing compound. The inlet valve cover must be replaced before the head is in place on the engine. Again check bevel positions.

As usual the head holding bolts should be tightened slowly and evenly. The bevel housing cover needs a new paper washer and procedure for refitting the shaft cover is the reverse of the dismantling process. If any oil leaks were apparent at either end of the shaft cover, a strand or two of asbestos string smeared with graphite grease should be wrapped round the cover inside each gland nut before it is screwed home.

Compression Plates. A word of warning should be given about these. If either is removed, a thinner top coupling for the vertical shaft must be substituted, otherwise the engine will be ruined.

Valve Timing. This should not have been lost if precautions have been taken along the lines previously indicated. If the setting is deranged, or it is desired to check it, one does this as follows: take out the sparking plug, and loosen the inlet valve cover nuts so as to raise this until the valve is visible. Engage the kick-start and rotate the engine until the inlet valve opens and closes. Insert through the sparking-plug orifice a piece of straight rod about 6 in. long and rest it on the top of the piston. Go on turning the engine over until top-dead-centre is reached. It may be necessary to repeat this a couple of times as the piston is often away on the downstroke before one realizes that T.D.C. has come and gone.

When T.D.C. is reached the slot in the top of the vertical cam-shaft drive ought to be exactly in line with the crankshaft, viewed as from the off side. Now the camshaft is rotated until the mark on the pinions register and the vertical marks on the shaft are similarly lined up. As previously described it may be necessary to turn the camshaft anything up to 21 turns, and the flywheel the same, to secure this alignment result.

Degree Timing. A timing disc attached to the engine shock absorber enables the alternative method of degree timing to be used. In this case the inlet valve opens 45° before T.D.C. and the exhaust *closes* 40° *after* T.D.C. Different timings are used on the KSS models (*see* page 70).

Retiming the Magneto. Having removed the chain cover, slacken the spindle nut and support the sprocket by inserting the shanks of two spanners behind it top and bottom. Remove the nut and tap the end of the spindle with a hammer and a soft drift (to avoid damaging the thread) to loosen the sprocket. Rotate the engine and with a rod in the plug-hole bring the piston up to $\frac{29}{64}$ in. of the top of the stroke with both valves closed. Fully advance the spark control and rotate the contact-breaker until the points open, the gap being 0·015 in. measured with a suitable feeler blade. Tighten the nut securing the bottom sprocket to the driving spindle. Recheck to make sure tightening the nut has not altered the contact-breaker position. Firing point is 40° before T.D.C. fully advanced.

MOV, MAC, and (early) MSS Models with Automatic Timing. MOV models, with the automatic timer at full retard, should have their contact-breaker points separating 9° before T.D.C. This is approximately $\frac{1}{32}$ in. of piston movement before T.D.C. and gives a maximum ignition advance of nearly 35° or $\frac{9}{32}$ in. With MAC and pre-1954 MSS models contact-breaker points should open 4° before T.D.C., giving a maximum advance of 32° or $\frac{11}{32}$ in. on the piston. By working to crankshaft degrees with a timing disc a greater standard of accuracy is ensured.

For the latest MSS a maximum advance of 36° is specified, with the automatic timing unit wedged or held (during the check) at full advance. The crankshaft is moved back until the points

DRIVING   **WEIGHTS**
GEAR

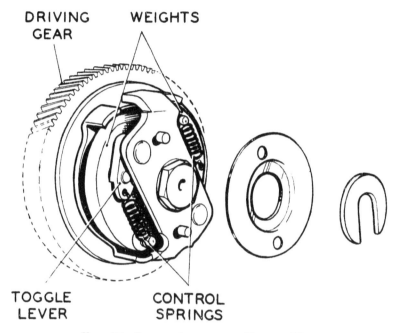

TOGGLE   **CONTROL**
LEVER   **SPRINGS**

FIG. 37. LUCAS AUTOMATIC TIMING UNIT
In fully retarded position.
(*By courtesy of Joseph Lucas Ltd.*)

are closed; a tissue-paper slip is then gripped between them. The crankshaft is now moved forward and the tissue should be freed at the 36° readings. For Viper, Venom and latest MAC the reading is 38°.

12 Clutch, Gearbox, and Cycle Parts

Engine Shaft Shock Absorber. Preparatory to dismantling this remove the dynamo belt cover, the front part of the rear chain cover, the rear chain and the outer half of the primary chain case. Pull out the split-pin from the crankshaft nut and with a ring spanner, or that provided by the makers, release the nut. The thread is right-handed and will probably have to be loosened with a blow from a mallet on the other end of the spanner.

When the nut is off, the dynamo drive pulley and shock absorber spring will come away. Between the mainshaft nut and the splines there is a plain washer. Next to come off is the shock absorber clutch. With the special spanner remove the sleeve gear locknut on the gearbox, and the complete clutch and engine sprocket are ready to withdraw together with the primary chain. Both sprockets must be taken off at once as the primary chain is endless. If difficulty is experienced in shifting the sleeve gear nut (it has a right-hand thread) put the machine in gear and apply the footbrake.

In reassembling, grease the engine sprocket and shock absorber clutch internally and also the splines, as the shock absorber must not be stiff in action. Tighten up the mainshaft nut hard against the plain washer, and do not be tempted to slacken it back to put in the split-pin (a new one).

Dismantling the Clutch. In taking this apart have a care for the three small thrust pins in the back plate. If the clutch is in good condition and has not been slipping, wash the linings in petrol and allow them to dry thoroughly before replacement.

The lining fabric should be $\frac{1}{32}$ in. proud of the steel plates though it will go on functioning until level. The ball-race must fit tightly in the chain sprocket but should move freely relative to the centre bearing of the back plate.

Reassembling the Clutch. Reassemble the back plate first, flat side down, then the steel ring with inserts, followed by the dished friction plate with the depressed part engaging the notches in the back plate. The chain wheel follows and a dished plate with projecting side up. The ring with the inserts engages with the notches on the chain wheel, and lastly the outer plate goes on.

This is a little difficult to fit as the notches must engage with the projections on the dished plate beneath. A little grease will hold the thrust pins in position on the back plate, to which they should be fitted.

The foregoing assembly is built up separately, then held together and placed upon the sleeve gear of the gearbox. Insert the 20 clutch springs in the adjusting ring. Clean and oil the sleeve gear locknut washers and put them in position. They take the slip as the nut is screwed up and prevent the clutch springs from doubling over. Tighten up the sleeve gear nut as much as possible, with the primary chain in place.

Worn friction plates should be exchanged for new ones. The fabric is pressed in and cannot be renewed manually.

The Clutch Cable. If there is any sign of fraying a new cable should be fitted. The tank has to come off and the old cable nipple is disengaged from the handlebar lever. Unscrew the cable stop holder from the gearbox, and remove and discard the old cable and cover. A complete new cable and cover, with nipples affixed, should be engaged first at the gearbox end. Adjust the clutch spring carrier so that the clutch slips when the engine is turned with the kick-start. Connect the nipple to the handlebar lever and set the adjuster so that there is no free movement in the cable. Place the new cover and cable in the clips to follow an easy curve. The tank can now be refitted, after which the clutch spring carrier is screwed out (anticlockwise) to give $\frac{3}{16}$ in. play at the lever. Work this fully to and fro while injecting a little penetrating oil into the cable cover. Recheck on the road to make sure slip has gone and not less then $\frac{3}{16}$ in. play remains in the cable.

If the rider is an expert with soldering, a broken or worn cable can be withdrawn and the cover used again but it is much better to get a new assembly. Amateur-soldered nipples are always apt to pull off.

Clutch Plate Adjustment. This is provided to compensate for wear or bedding down of linings. Stand the machine and remove the front part of the rear chain cover (attached by a stud to the primary cover and telescoped into the rear part of the rear chain cover). The clutch adjusting tool, a rod, is engaged through the sprocket with one of the serrations in the clutch spring carrier. If the spring carrier is pulled round backwards (anti-clockwise) tendency to clutch slip is decreased. Conversely turning clockwise frees the clutch. The adjustment is made with the gearbox in neutral by turning the rear wheel in the required direction. It is important to maintain the $\frac{3}{16}$ in. free movement on the cable,

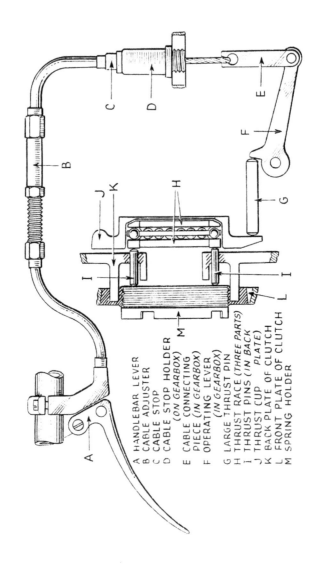

A HANDLEBAR LEVER
B CABLE ADJUSTER
C CABLE STOP
D CABLE STOP HOLDER
  (ON GEARBOX)
E CABLE CONNECTING
  PIECE (IN GEARBOX)
F OPERATING LEVER
  (IN GEARBOX)
G LARGE THRUST PIN
H THRUST RACE (THREE PARTS)
I THRUST PINS (IN BACK
  PLATE)
J THRUST CUP
K BACK PLATE OF CLUTCH
L FRONT PLATE OF CLUTCH
M SPRING HOLDER

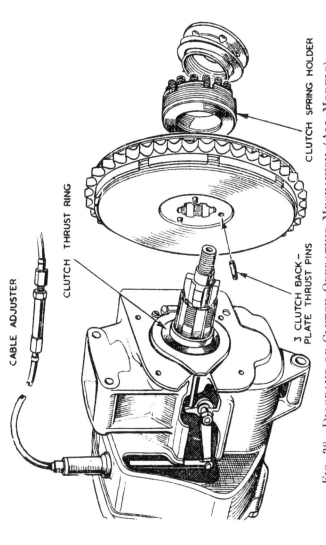

CABLE ADJUSTER

CLUTCH THRUST RING

CLUTCH SPRING HOLDER

3 CLUTCH BACK-
PLATE THRUST PINS

FIG. 38. DIAGRAMS OF CLUTCH OPERATING MECHANISM (ALL MODELS)

(*By courtesy of "Motor Cycle"*)

previously mentioned, otherwise the clutch thrust race will be
overloaded.

Stripping and Reassembling the Gearbox. This is only necessary
if trouble develops. Drain the oil when warm. Take out the three
bolts securing the kick-start housing, and draw this away with
the crank and ratchet. Unless a new spring is to be fitted these

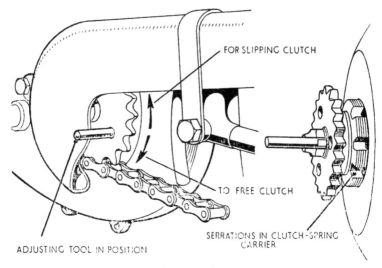

FOR SLIPPING CLUTCH

TO FREE CLUTCH

SERRATIONS IN CLUTCH-SPRING
CARRIER

ADJUSTING TOOL IN POSITION

FIG. 39. CLUTCH ADJUSTMENT

need not be disturbed. Unscrew the gearshaft-end-bearing cap
and remove the hexagon nut from the end of the shaft. Take off
the secondary chain cover and the chain. Return to the gearshaft
and tap this about an inch into the box.

Unscrew all the end-cover bolts and disconnect the gear rod
from the outside striking lever. The nuts on the ends of the
selector bars which project through the end cover can be removed,
and when these are off the cover comes away. Getting out the
selector bars requires a $\frac{3}{8}$ in. steel template to span the housing
and a number of packing washers so that when the nuts are
refitted over these the bars will be withdrawn.

Low gear can be pulled off, and the gearshaft from the clutch
end. The middle gear and its striking fork then come away. The
bottom selector fork is raised to disengage the peg from the cam
plate track, freeing layshaft and fork. The two layshaft end gears
are removable only by a press. The layshaft driving gear can only
be disengaged in one position (found by rotating the layshaft)
because the teeth on the top gear "pick-up" mask the sleeve gear

teeth at all points but one. After reassembly, the box should be refilled with engine oil, the level plug being removed to allow the oil just to run from it, when filling is stopped and the plug replaced.

Renewing the Kick-start Spring. With the housing off, knock out the cotter after the kick-start nut has been removed. The spring anchor peg comes out of the top of the housing and the crank can be released from the end of the ratchet. One loop of the new spring goes over the peg in the ratchet, after which ratchet and spring

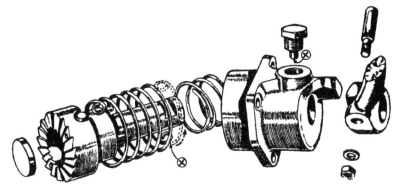

FIG. 40. KICK-START RATCHET AND SPRINGS
(*By courtesy of "Motor Cycling," London*)

are positioned in the housing so that the other loop of the spring is below the anchor pin hole in the housing.

Next, after verifying that the thrust pins and the engaging spring are in position, the anchor peg is adjusted till its projection engages with the spring loop. Now, by holding the large end of the ratchet in a vice, the starter spring can be wound into tension, when it only remains to refit the crank, replace the cotter, and mount the complete housing again on the gearbox end cover. The thrust washer must be in place on the ratchet and the threaded part of the kick-start cotter faces the rear of the machine.

Front Chain Adjustment. Three bolts secure the gearbox to the engine plate and these are slackened. To tighten the chain the nuts at the offside of the gearbox are moved forward along the adjuster, causing the gearbox to be drawn backwards. There is an inspection hole in the primary chain case and the chain tension should be checked through this. The tightest point that can be found, turning the chain to a number of positions, should have a deflection of $\frac{3}{8}$ in. After retightening the gearbox bolts, check the adjustment again and then lock the adjuster.

Adjusting the Secondary Chain. The rear wheel spindle is loosened but not excessively. If the alignment of the wheel is known to be accurate the chain adjuster lock-nuts can be released and the adjusters screwed in exactly evenly until the chain has a deflection of ¾ in. at the tightest point that can be found on the lower centre run. The adjustment should be made a very little at a time or alignment will be lost.

If the alignment is suspect a straight-edge about 7 ft long, which can be a plank with one edge planed dead straight, should be laid along both wheels as high up as the mudguards will allow. If tyres of equal size are fitted and properly inflated the straight-edge should touch both tyres front and rear. Wrong alignment must be remedied by patient readjustment, remembering that the secondary chain tension must be corrected at the same time.

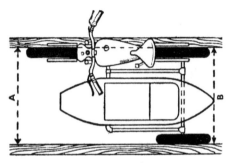

FIG. 41. SIDECAR ALIGNMENT

DISTANCE *A* SHOULD BE ¾ IN. LESS THAN *B* FOR PROPER TOE-IN

Sidecar Alignment. After correcting chain and wheel line-up on the machine the sidecar should be tracked up. Another straight-edge is required and is laid against the sidecar wheel while the first straight-edge is held against the motor-cycle wheels at the offside. The two boards must be raised to exactly the same height, this being as high as it is possible to lift the board on the offside of the machine. The distances between the inside edges of the boards, measured as close as possible to the tyres, should be ¾ in. less at the front than at the back. This "toe-in" makes the wheels run parallel.

All spindle- and lock-nut alignment points should be rechecked after tightening up. Alignments are liable to be disordered by movement caused in tightening these nuts.

Removing the Rear Wheel. On camshaft models undo the nuts securing the rear stand to the mudguard extension and pull the

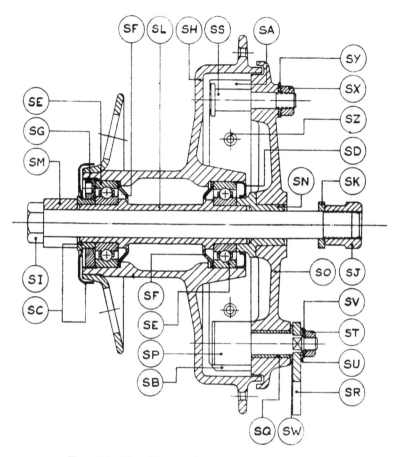

FIG. 42. THE FRONT HUB—SECTIONAL VIEW

SA = Brake shoes.
SB = Brake shoe slipper.
SC = Outer dust cap and sleeve.
SD = Inner dust cap.
SE = Ballraces.
SF = Grease retainers.
SG = Ballrace retaining ring.
SH = Front hub shell.
SI = Detachable spindle.
SJ = Nut for detachable spindle.
SK = Washer for spindle nut.
SL = Hollow spindle.
SM = Split sleeve for spindle.

SN = Bearing clamping sleeve.
SO = Brake plate.
SP = Brake cam.
SQ = Bush for brake cam.
SR = Lever for brake cam.
SS = Fulcrum pin.
ST = Nut for cam.
SU = Square-hole washer for cam.
SV = Lock washer.
SW = Felt washer for cam.
SX = Nut for fulcrum pin.
SY = Plain washer for fulcrum pin.
SZ = Brake shoe spring.

Hub Lubrication: Mobil Hub Grease; Retinax A or H; Duckham's H.B.B. Grease
Energrease C.3; Castrolease Heavy; Esso Multi Purpose Grease "H."

(By courtesy Veloce Ltd.)

95

machine on to the stand. The rear mudguard extension must be taken away by loosening the bolts holding it to the guard, and by undoing the rear lamp. The inner flange on the wheel is fastened by three nuts to studs on the brake drum and these are removed with a box spanner. Unscrew the spindle from the off side of the machine and remove the distance piece. The wheel can now be detached. These models have journal bearings. Each 10,000 miles

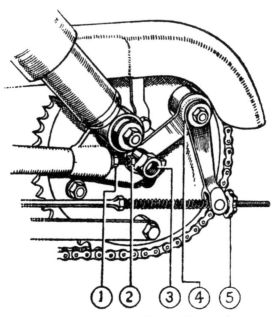

FIG. 43. REAR BRAKE AND REAR CHAIN ADJUSTMENT

1. Chain adjuster lock-nut.
2. Chain adjuster.
3. Rear brake plate locking-bolt nut.
4. Rear brake cam felt washer.
5. Rear brake adjusting nut.

Never check the chain tension when the chain is in motion—this is highly dangerous.

they should be removed and packed with high melting point grease. These bearings are non-adjustable and when worn must be renewed.

Brake Adjustment. That of the front brake is made by releasing the lock-ring near the bottom of the forks and tightening the adjuster until play is removed but leaving the wheel to spin free. Retighten the lock-ring. The rear brake has a plated hexagon nut on the end of the rod. When the levers have passed the 90° mark on either brake the ends of the brake shoes, where they bear on the cams, may be padded with U-shaped iron packing pieces.

Brake linings once fouled with oil or grease cannot be restored and the shoes, as with worn linings, can be exchanged at the dealer for relined shoes. The amateur will find the sticking on and riveting of new linings very difficult, and the incidental risks are too great.

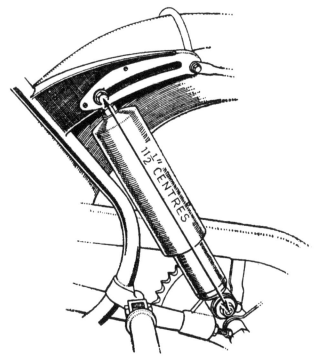

FIG. 44. REAR SUSPENSION—ADJUSTMENT FOR LOAD

Rear suspension unit compressed to mid-position for adjusting rear chain
The suspension is shown adjusted for solo riding, with pivot bolts right
forward in slots.

Telescopic Forks. Two types of these forks have been used; earlier, the Dowty, a pneumatic assembly entirely air-supported and inflated by applying a pump to a Kilner valve at the top of the near-side tube. A balance pipe keeps both tubes at the same pressure.

Velocette Spring-damped Forks. These are fitted to MAC machines from 1951 onwards, as well as to all current models, and are non-inflatable. Each fork leg holds $\frac{1}{8}$ pint of SAE20 oil.

Steering Head Adjustment. Support the machine under the engine so that the front wheel is free. Slacken the nut on the fork head clip bolt and tighten down the column lock-nut until there is no play but the steering is still perfectly free. If any roughness is felt the ball races should be removed by drawing out the column. Each race holds 19 balls and sets of all new balls should be fitted.

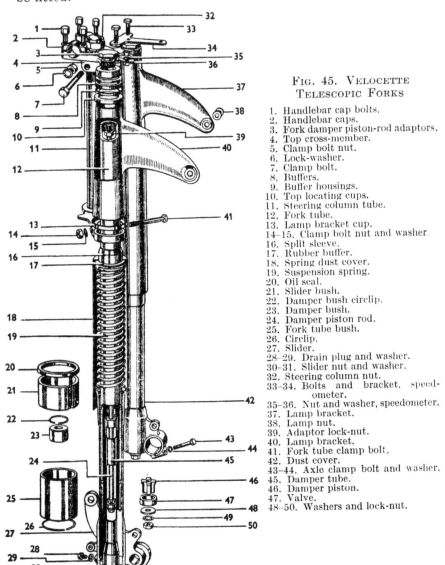

FIG. 45. VELOCETTE TELESCOPIC FORKS

1. Handlebar cap bolts.
2. Handlebar caps.
3. Fork damper piston-rod adaptors.
4. Top cross-member.
5. Clamp bolt nut.
6. Lock-washer.
7. Clamp bolt.
8. Buffers.
9. Buffer housings.
10. Top locating cups.
11. Steering column tube.
12. Fork tube.
13. Lamp bracket cup.
14-15. Clamp bolt nut and washer.
16. Split sleeve.
17. Rubber buffer.
18. Spring dust cover.
19. Suspension spring.
20. Oil seal.
21. Slider bush.
22. Damper bush circlip.
23. Damper bush.
24. Damper piston rod.
25. Fork tube bush.
26. Circlip.
27. Slider.
28-29. Drain plug and washer.
30-31. Slider nut and washer.
32. Steering column nut.
33-34. Bolts and bracket, speedometer.
35-36. Nut and washer, speedometer.
37. Lamp bracket.
38. Lamp nut.
39. Adaptor lock-nut.
40. Lamp bracket.
41. Fork tube clamp bolt,
42. Dust cover.
43-44. Axle clamp bolt and washer.
45. Damper tube.
46. Damper piston.
47. Valve.
48-50. Washers and lock-nut.

13 The Electrical System

Two types of electrical and ignition systems are used on single-cylinder Velocettes. The GTP two-stroke model had coil ignition plus dynamo and battery for lighting. On four-stroke models there is a separate magneto for ignition.

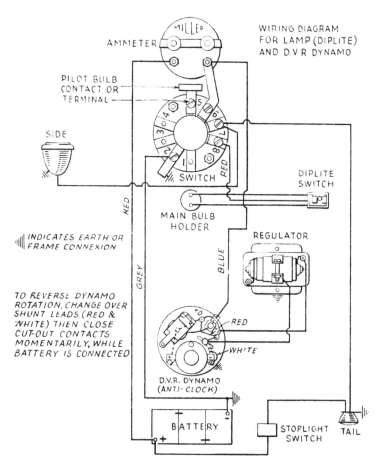

FIG. 46. MILLER GENERAL CIRCUIT DIAGRAM
(SINGLE-CYLINDER MODELS)

Battery Maintenance. Regularly inspect the battery liquid or electrolyte, once a month to once a week depending on the time of year, the amount of use of the machine, and the warmth or otherwise of the weather. The electrolyte level should be kept just above the tops of the plates, but no more. Distilled water, at a

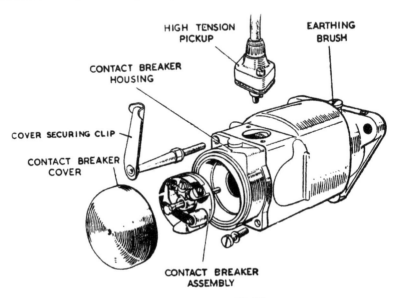

FIG. 47. LUCAS-TYPE KIF MAGNETO

few pence from the chemist's, is added. Non-spill or so called "dry" accumulators should be topped-up with distilled water until the top of the fibrous filling is saturated.

Combustible gas emanates from the battery particularly when it is fully charged and "fizzing", so naked lights should never be used for inspection. Clear corrosion off the terminals and smear them with petroleum jelly. Lack of attention to the battery is the cause of most lighting and coil ignition troubles.

Testing. The best test of a battery's condition is that given by a hydrometer, which also serves as a convenient instrument for refilling it without splashing. Insert the nozzle of the hydrometer and draw up electrolyte into the bulb till the float is free. A well-charged battery should read 1·285 to 1·300. The half-charge reading is about 1·210 and full discharge 1·150. All three cells should read the same; if they do not it is an indication that the low one is weak and will overstrain the others.

Storage. If the motor-cycle is to be laid up for the winter or for any period, the battery must be removed and given a freshening charge once a fortnight. A battery allowed to discharge and left will soon be ruined.

Miller Headlamp 179CV, For Viper, Venom, MSS, etc.

The headlamp is fitted with one bifocal bulb and one parking (pilot) bulb. The types used are—

Headlamp bulb: 6-volt 30 × 24 watt (MAC, 24 × 24 watt). Double filament, bifocal prefocussed type (MAC, s.b.c. cap).
Pilot bulb: 6-volt 3 watt. Single filament. M.e.s. cap (MAC, s.c.c. cap).

To remove the lamp front to change a bulb or for other attention, free the clip below the lamp rim and pull the rim away from the lamp from the bottom first. Before doing work to the switch involving any connexions, always take the cables off the positive battery terminal.

The bulbs are detachable from the back of the reflector after removing the bayonet-fixed contact assembly to which the leads are attached. To remove the lamp glass and reflector unit release the four—or more—fixing clips from under the lip of the headlamp rim. The unit will then come out of the rim. Do not touch the highly polished inside optical surface of the reflector with fingertips or anything else.

When replacing the reflector see that it is fitted correctly with the opening for the pilot bulb uppermost. Refit the lamp front at the top first; push it over the lower edge and engage the fixing clip. On Viper and Venom models the rear and stop lamps are combined and the bulb is a 6-volt 18 × 6 watt offset-pin stop-light bulb. To remove the bulb take out the two screws from the plastic case and take this off.

The Dynamo Brushes. Before taking off the dynamo cover to get at the brushes disconnect the positive battery lead to prevent a short circuit. Each brush is held in position by a spring lever and if this is lifted aside the brush can be pulled out of its holder. Deal with each separately to avoid any possibility of their getting replaced in the wrong slots.

Movement of each brush in its holder should be free but not sloppy. The curved surface bedding down on the commutator should present a smooth polish, and if there are ridges on the brushes this is a sign that the commutator needs skimming. The brushes, of course, gradually wear down and it is advisable to replace them when the tops of the brushes are appreciably below the level of the holders.

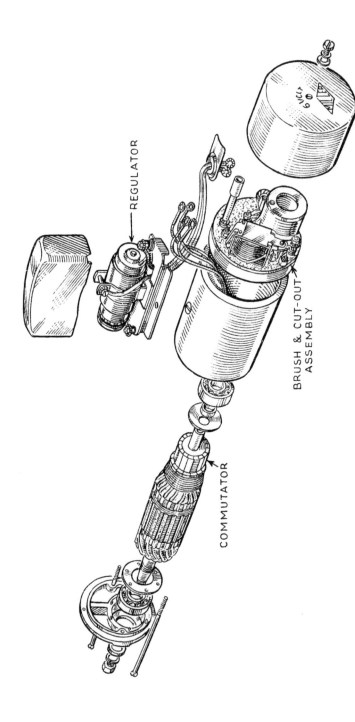

REGULATOR

BRUSH & CUT-OUT ASSEMBLY

COMMUTATOR

Fig. 48. Exploded View of Miller Dynamo

The Commutator. This tends, as just mentioned, to wear into ridges, to become blackened, and to fill, as to the space between the bars, with hardened dust from the brushes. Any or all of these conditions seriously affect the current output. Little can really be done with the commutator in position. If the owner understands the fairly simple process of stripping the dynamo he had best take out the armature. The commutator bars can then be undercut to expose but not damage the mica insulation, after which the bars should be skimmed and polished. New brushes will complete a good job.

The Cut-out. This automatic device prevents the current from the battery passing backwards through the dynamo windings. The points therefore close when the dynamo voltage rises above that of the battery and open when it drops again. If there is any trouble with the cut-out the makers should be asked to recondition it.

The Ammeter. This will always serve as a reliable indicator of health in the electrical system. If the needle constantly flickers while indicating charge, the fault, if not traceable to anything obvious such as a loose connexion, will indicate bad commutation: worn brushes, rough bars, and so on. The vibration to which a motor-cycle is subject renders it desirable to pay immediate heed to any abnormal indication from the needle. Modern wiring is mostly insulated with trouble-free plastic sheathing, but older machines with rubber insulation are prone to mishaps due to rotted rubber. Dynamo wires may be shorted by oil-soaked insulation.

A sudden swing to full discharge, with the needle running off the scale, indicates such a short and the rider should stop and switch off as quickly as possible, immediately disconnecting the battery.

With the wiring diagrams and trouble-tables (*see* pp. 113–15) no difficulty should be experienced in locating and remedying any electrical defects.

14 The Amal Carburettor

THE working of this needle-jet instrument is made plain from the accompanying illustration. When the petrol tap is turned on fuel flows past a valve controlled by the float, lifting this until, in the fully raised position, the valve shuts off the supply. As fuel is used the float drops and the valve reopens, the process of rising and falling being entirely automatic. The rider should never alter the float level.

Fuel passes from the float chamber through diagonal holes in the jet plug to communicate with the main jet and the pilot feed, keeping the level in both the same as in the float chamber. If the throttle is only slightly open the partial vacuum draws air through the pilot-air hole and a small quantity of air/petrol mixture is sprayed into the engine through the pilot feed. This is the idling condition.

As the throttle is opened the suction on the pilot feed decreases and a second pilot passage, farther back in the carburettor, supplements the supply. When the throttle is about $\frac{1}{8}$ open the main jet begins to experience suction, the extent being governed by the throttle cutaway up to the $\frac{1}{4}$-throttle position. From here to $\frac{3}{4}$-throttle mixture regulation depends upon the position of the rising needle. Past $\frac{3}{4}$-throttle, however, the unobstructed main jet takes charge.

An air slide, cable-operated from the handlebar on two-lever carburettors and hand-operated on single-lever types, obstructs the main through-way. This increases the suction on the main jet and enrichens the mixture. The operation of the air slide is partially, but not entirely, the same as that of what is commonly called a choke or strangler control.

Tuning. Shown in Fig. 52 on page 109 there are four tuning sequences in an Amal carburettor as indicated two paragraphs previously. The pilot screw with its two passages (closed throttle to $\frac{1}{8}$ open) controls idling. The cutaway on the air intake side of the throttle block is in charge up to $\frac{1}{4}$-throttle. From here to $\frac{3}{4}$-throttle the needle position is the factor. Thereafter the size of the main jet determines performance.

If the correct jet and other sizes have been altered or lost it will simplify tuning if the assistance of Amal Ltd., Holford Works, Perry Bar, Birmingham, 20, is first sought. Give the engine number of the model and ask for standard settings when writing to them.*

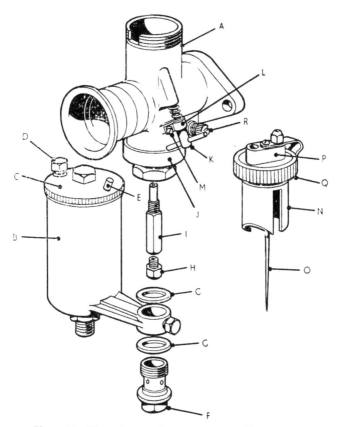

FIG. 49. THE AMAL CARBURETTOR (EXPLODED)

A = Body.	J = Brass union.
B = Float chamber.	K = Throttle stop.
C = Float chamber lid.	L = Lock clip.
D = Lock-nut.	M = Clip screw.
E = Flooder.	N = Throttle sleeve.
F = Jet plug.	O = Needle.
GG = Fibre washers.	P = Cable housing.
H = Main jet.	Q = Throttle assembly ring.
I = Needle jet.	R = Pilot jet adjuster.

The Pilot Adjuster. Make sure the air passages are unobstructed as frequently the small holes become partly filled with impacted dust and a smooth tickover cannot be obtained whatever the position of the pilot screw. The correct setting of the screw

* *See also page* 108.

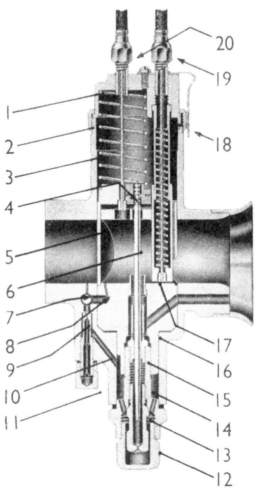

Fig. 50. Sectional View of Amal Monobloc
Carburettor

1. Mixing-chamber cap.
2. Mixing-chamber lock ring.
3. Body.
4. Taper-needle grooves.
5. Throttle valve.
6. Taper needle.
7. By-pass.
8. Pilot outlet.
9. Pilot jet.
10. Pilot-jet passage.
11. Pilot-jet cap.
12. Main-jet plug.
13. Main jet.
14. Needle-jet sleeve.
15. Needle jet.
16. Jet block.
17. Air valve.
18. Clip.
19.⎫ Cable adjusters.
20.⎭

106

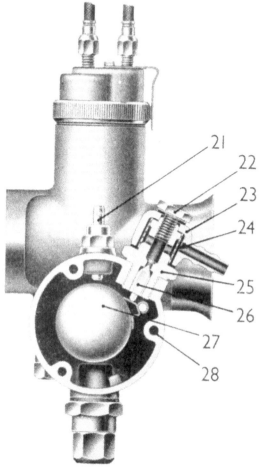

FIG. 51. AMAL MONOBLOC CARBURETTOR SHOWING
DETAILS OF FLOAT CHAMBER

21. Flooder button.
22. Petrol-union cap.
23. Petrol-union banjo.
24. Petrol inlet.

25. Petrol-union locknut.
26. Needle valve.
27. Float.
28. Float-chamber cover screw orifice.

VELOCETTE AMAL CARBURETTORS

(By courtesy of Amal Ltd.)

Type No.	Veloce Ref.	Model	Main Jet	Throttle Valve	Needle Jet Size and Position	Pilot Jet (c.c.)	Banjo	Bore Size of Carburettor (in.)
276EY/1AT	—	MAC 350	130	6/4	107 (3)	—	—	1 5/16
376/48	A29/14	MAC 350	200	376/3½	1055 (3)	25	—	1 5/16
376/61	A29/18	Viper 350	270	376/3½	106 (3)	30	—	1 1/16
T10TT9	A29/26	Viper 350	360	7	109 (4)	—	14/250	1 1/16
T10GP	A29/27	Viper 350	220	4	109 (3)	—	14/250	1 1/16
T10TT9	A29/25	Viper 350 (Std. silencer)	340	4	109 (3)	—	14/250	1 1/16
376/49	A29/15	MSS 500 (Endurance)	240	376/3½	1055 (3)	25	—	1 1/8
T10TT9	A29/13	MSS 500 (Scrambler)	420	7	109 (4)	—	14/250	1 1/8
389/15	A29/19	Venom 500	330	389/3½	106 (4)	30	—	1 3/16
T10TT9	A29/23	Venom 500	390	5	109 (3)	—	14/250	1 3/16
T10TT9	A29/22	Venom 500 Clubman	370	4	109 (3)	—	14/250	1 3/16
T10GP	A29/24	Venom 500	240	4	109 (2)	—	14/250	1 3/16
363/1 363/7	LAS 8/42 LAS 84/5	LE 200 (192 c.c.)	65	363/2	1045 (3)	15	360/036	0·475
363/4(L)/5(R)	LAS 214 (84/3 + 84/4)	(Valiant (192 c.c.)	100 (both)	2 (both)	1045 (3) (both)	15 (both)	—	5/8
376/259	TAS 84	Viceroy 248 c.c.	210	376/3	1055 (3)	25	376/097	1 1/16

Settings for any model not listed here can be obtained from Amal Ltd., Holford Works, Perry Bar, Birmingham, 20.

is $1\frac{1}{2}$ to 2 turns open from the fully closed position. Alter in conjunction with the throttle-stop screw until an even tickover is reached.

Too much throttle cutaway leads to spitting back in moving away from the idling position, the mixture being too weak. Too little cutaway gives lumpy running but no spitting back, indicating the mixture is too rich.

The needle should be as low as possible. There are five grooves in needles fitted to the two-lever carburettor, and tuning can

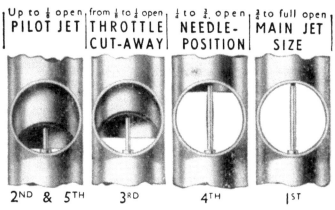

Up to $\frac{1}{8}$ open	from $\frac{1}{8}$ to $\frac{1}{4}$ open	$\frac{1}{4}$ to $\frac{3}{4}$ open	$\frac{3}{4}$ to full open
PILOT JET	THROTTLE CUT-AWAY	NEEDLE-POSITION	MAIN JET SIZE
2ND & 5TH	3RD	4TH	1ST

FIG. 52. AMAL TUNING SEQUENCE

start with the spring clip in the centre groove. The lower the needle sits the weaker the mixture. Do not alter the position by more than one groove at a time.

It is certain that in an old machine the needle jet will need replacement, especially if it is of the obsolete bronze type. A stainless steel needle jet can now be obtained which is practically unwearable. The needle itself is less likely to wear, but the size should be verified with Amal Ltd.

All moving parts in the carburettor wear with the passing of time and good performance and tuning cannot be retained if worn components are retained. Accurate tuning is impossible with a bent needle, a worn throttle-block loose in its housing, or air leaks at the junction of carburettor and engine.

15 Overhaul Hints

OVERHAUL of a secondhand machine along the lines generally indicated in this book can be greatly helped by a little "know-how" of the type familiar to the old hand but less so to the novice. Many small tips have been given in the preceding chapters but here are a few more.

Tight Bearings. Ball or roller bearings tightly fitting in aluminium housings should never be forced out cold, but warmed slightly. This can be done with care over a gas flame. Too much heat will, of course, ruin the bearing. If, conversely, the bearing turns in the housing a thin film of solder applied to the outside of the bearing shell will effect a cure, or the aluminium (which will only take solder itself if the right type is used) can be cautiously caulked with a flat punch.

Exhaust Nuts. These are frequently obstinate. Never try to force a heat-bound nut, but wrap it in a paraffin-soaked rag and leave overnight. Penetrating oil will also help by creeping into the stuck threads.

Spring Links. Since chains cannot be stretched, the spring link must always be fitted by holding the two ends in adjoining sprocket valleys. Where there is insufficient clearance to introduce the link, which must be pushed in from the rear, slack the chain fully and tie a length of stout string through the links. If this is twisted up tourniquet fashion the link can sometimes be drawn close enough for the U-piece to be inserted in the free run. In putting the spring clip in position always have its rounded nose (closed end) pointing forward, in the direction of the run.

Sparking Plugs. Any detachable or non-detachable type plug can now be quickly cleaned at a garage on an "air blast" service unit, all deposits removed, and the plug tested for sparking at over 100 lb per sq in. If you dismantle a plug, it should be gripped in a vice just tightly enough to secure it. Over the gland of the plug pass a ring spanner or a plug box spanner.

Scrape out deposits from within the body with the small blade of an old penknife. Brush the points clean with a fine wire brush. Scrape the centre electrode and the insulator, rub if necessary with worn emery cloth, and finally clean both centre and body with a petrol-damped rag. In reassembling see that the dished copper washer upon which the centre electrode beds down is present and undamaged, applying a trace of graphited grease to the lower surface of the insulator at the bedding point.

Tap the outer electrode or electrodes, or set them with a pair of long-nosed pliers or a gapping tool, to 0·02 in. from the centre electrode. Never in any circumstances bend this to set the gap. The thickness of the thumbnail is sometimes a rough measure of the correct gap. If the plug is suspect lay it on a metal part of the engine and with the machine in shadow kick the engine over (with the ignition switched on if coil ignition is fitted). If a good spark is not visible at the plug points after overhaul the plug must be scrapped. Sometimes a plug will spark out of the engine but not under compression, so this test is not infallible.

Sparking Plug Types. The early GTP and K models used an 18 mm plug, of which the M60KLG, H1 Lodge, or 17 Champion are suitable. The K models use a 16 Champion, but the Mk. II Ks (14 mm) use FE80 KLG, HLN Lodge, or NA8 Champion.

Post-1935 GTPs and all later Velocette single-cylinder models have 14 mm plugs, and early MOV and MAC models also use F70KLG, H14 Lodge, or L105 Champion. Alloy-head MAC models require longer-reach plugs (FE70 KLG, HLN Lodge, or NA8 Champion). MSS models of early type can use F80 KLG, HN Lodge, L115 Champion; latest MSS machines take long-reach plugs such as FE80 KLG, HLN/HLNP Lodge, NA8 Champion. (For the twin-cylinder models: LEs and Valiants, 10 mm long-reach, *see* page 19. Viceroy Scooter, 14 mm KLG FE50 or FE80, Champion N8, N3, Lodge CLN, 2HLNY). NGK plugs are O.K.

Tyres. The following table should be faithfully adhered to in regard to tyre pressures. Under- or over-inflation will shorten the

Minimum Inflation Pressures	TYRE SECTION	
	3·00 in.	3·25 in.
lb and kg	LOAD PER WHEEL IN LB	
16 (1·2)	160	200
18 (1·3)	180	240
20 (1·4)	200	280
24 (1·8)	240	350
28 (2·0)	300	400
32 (2·3)	350	440

life of tyres. Regularly inspect the covers as well and prise out any flints, chips of glass, or nails embedded in the treads.

Removing a Cover. This is quite easy if the correct drill is followed. Assuming the wheel has been removed, take out the valve core and unscrew the lock-nut, if fitted, from the valve base. Push the valve right inside the cover. Press the cover wall down into the well by the valve. At the opposite side of the tyre introduce a spoon lever underneath the bead and lift it away from the rim. Have a second lever handy and introduce this under the

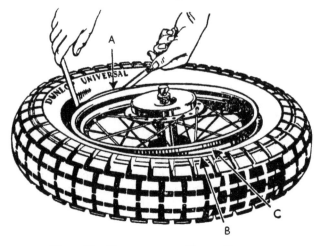

FIG. 53. REMOVING A TYRE COVER

bead about 4–5 in. from the first one. Check very carefully that the tube is not nipped under either lever, and press both down towards the hub so that several inches of the cover are drawn over the rim. If necessary remove one lever and reinsert it 2–3 in. farther along. The bead will yield and can be drawn over the rim with the fingers.

Pull out the tube, locate the puncture and roughen the area for an inch or so all round. Apply a thin coating of solution and let dry completely. Strip off the backing from a patch big enough to cover the hole with half an inch to spare all round, avoiding contact between the prepared rubber and the fingers. Touch one end down over the edge of the solutioned area and roll the patch on flat. If the patch puckers wet it with petrol, strip off, scrap the patch and start again with a new one.

If the patch sticks flat press it well down and dust over the area with french chalk. Before reinserting the tube in the cover carefully feel round the inside for the source of the puncture and get rid of it, or the tyre will soon be punctured again. Tuck the tube back into the cover with the utmost care to avoid folding or twisting it. Inflate slightly to verify this, deflate, and fit the wall by the valve first. It should be possible to replace the whole cover wall without recourse to levers.

Choked Silencer. This can be an unsuspected source of trouble, severe loss of power and a "hollow" exhaust being symptoms. The simplest way of clearing a choked silencer is to take it off, stop up one end with a wooden plug, stand it on this end, and fill it with a solution of caustic soda. Used in the strength of one pound (anhydrous) sifted slowly into a gallon of water, this will loosen and bring away the carbon overnight. Dump the caustic into an unwanted corner of the garden as it must not be emptied into the drains. Flush out thoroughly with water, warm or cold.

Fault Diagnosis. The following tables will be found useful. In each case the suggestions progress from "most likely" to "least likely" and if worked through systematically the cure will be found:

ENGINE REFUSES TO START

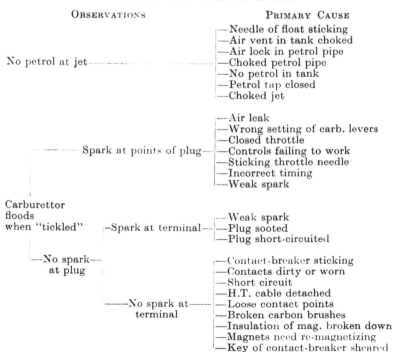

OBSERVATIONS	PRIMARY CAUSE
No petrol at jet	—Needle of float sticking —Air vent in tank choked —Air lock in petrol pipe —Choked petrol pipe —No petrol in tank —Petrol tap closed —Choked jet
Spark at points of plug	—Air leak —Wrong setting of carb. levers —Closed throttle —Controls failing to work —Sticking throttle needle —Incorrect timing —Weak spark
Carburettor floods when "tickled" —Spark at terminal	—Weak spark —Plug sooted —Plug short-circuited
—No spark— at plug ——No spark at terminal	—Contact-breaker sticking —Contacts dirty or worn —Short circuit —H.T. cable detached —Loose contact points —Broken carbon brushes —Insulation of mag. broken down —Magnets need re-magnetizing —Key of contact-breaker sheared

ELECTRICAL FAULTS

Condition	Possible Causes and Methods of Detection	Remedy
	Bulb filament broken.	Replace with new bulb.
	Bulb discoloured with use.	Do.
	Bulb out of focus.	Focus the bulb until the best illumination is obtained.
	Severed or worn cable, or loose connexions at headlamp switch, dynamo, or battery.	Tighten loose connexions and replace faulty cables.
Lamps give dim, flickering, or no light when the engine is not running.	Faulty earthing of headlamp. The earthing lead from the lamp or switch must be securely connected to the earthing on "Magdyno."	Do.
	Faulty earthing of battery. The cable from the negative battery terminal must be securely connected to a metal part of the machine.	Do.
	Battery exhausted. Take hydrometer readings when acid level is correct and after a run when electrolyte is thoroughly mixed. When half discharged, readings are about 1·210. When fully discharged readings are about 1·150.	Machine should be taken on the road for a long daytime run with switch in "C" position, or battery charged from independent electrical supply.
	Dynamo not charging, or charging intermittently. Ammeter should give a reading on the charge side when the machine is running at say 20 m.p.h., with switch in "C" position. Possible causes of dynamo trouble are—	
	Loose connexions at headlamp switch, dynamo, or battery.	Tighten loose connexions.
	Faulty contacts in headlamp switch.	Examine spring triggers and see that they make good contact with terminals.
After carrying out examination lamps still give dim, flickering, or no light when the engine is running.	Worn or dirty brushes.	Clean dirty or greasy brushes with a cloth moistened with petrol. Badly worn brushes must be replaced.
	Dirty commutator.	To clean dirty commutator, remove one of the main brushes from its holder and insert a fine duster holding it pressed against the commutator surface by means of a suitably shaped piece of wood, at the same time slowly turning the engine. If commutator has been badly neglected, clean with very fine glass-paper.
	Reversed polarity of dynamo.	To correct polarity of machine run engine slowly, put switch in "C" position, and then press cut-out contacts momentarily together.

MISFIRING

Condition	Possible Causes and Methods of Detection	Remedy
Engine will not fire or fires erratically.	Remove plug and allow to rest on cylinder head. If a spark occurs at plug points when engine is slowly turned over, the ignition equipment is O.K.	Look for engine defects and check ignition timing.
	If no spark occurs at plug points remove lead and plug, replace with new length of cable and test independently of plug by holding cable end about ¼ in. from metal part of engine. If magneto sparks, H.T. lead or plug is faulty.	Replace H.T. cable if perished or cracked. Clean plug electrodes, adjust gap to about 20 thousandths of an inch.
	If magneto does not spark, possible causes of trouble are—Contact-breaker gap out of adjustment and contacts dirty.	Clean dirty or pitted contacts with fine caborundum stone or fine emery cloth and afterwards with a cloth moistened with petrol. Verify timing first. To adjust gap, turn engine slowly until the points are seen to be fully opened, then slacken locking nut and rotate fixed contact screw by its hexagon head until the gap is set to thickness of gauge.
	Contact-breaker rocker arm sticking.	Remove contact-breaker, and prise rocker arm off its bearing. Clean steel pin if necessary with fine emery cloth and then, having removed all grit, moisten with a few drops of oil before replacing the lever.
	Pick-up brush worn or broken.	Fit new brush. Before fitting, clean slip ring track.

16 Trials and Scrambles

HIGH performance is obtainable from Venom and Viper Sports and Clubman models after they have been carefully run-in. For the rider who wishes to do a little better still, instructions are issued by Veloce Ltd. in their service literature and have been condensed into the following hints (by kind permission of the company). They form a series of suggested steps which can be taken, after running-in, to give superlative performance. Many of the suggestions are of course applicable to all motor-cycles as well as to Velocette machines.

Racing Equipment. Carburettors and magnetos of racing type, and rev. counters, are available from the makers for standard Viper and Venom models. The Service Department will supply a list. A great deal can first be done to improve performance or restore lost power.

Eliminating Avoidable Friction. Power can be lost between the engine and the wheels, particularly, of course, the rear wheel, and this loss must be reduced to the minimum as a first step. Raise and spin the wheels. Brake shoes should completely clear the drum when the pedal, or lever, is released. Operate the brakes several times, noting any signs of sluggish action such as binding cam spindles.

Driving chains must be in good condition, lubricated, adjusted and aligned. Venom Clubman and Scrambler models have the driving side rear engine plate reinforced to prevent the primary chain line deflecting under very heavy load. The reinforced plate can be fitted to the Viper, or earlier models.

Tyre pressures must follow the maker's recommendations. Otherwise power is lost; the tyres themselves will suffer, as will steering and road holding. Power loss in the gearbox is reduced by use of the correct grade of oil and avoiding over-filling.

The Clutch Adjustment. This is most important as the slightest slip on full throttle will drop maximum speed by several miles an hour. Such slip may not be noticeable under normal conditions. Check, as follows, that there is enough play in the thrust bearing for the springs to exert full pressure on the linings—

1. Fully slacken the midway cable adjuster and slip the cable nipple out of the handlebar lever.

2. With full-open throttle and air controls, and gears in neutral, operate the kick-start against compression. If the clutch slips, omit the next step and go straight to number four.

3. Engage the clutch adjusting tool in the spring holder and pull the rear wheel backwards a little at a time. Check for clutch slip after each movement, taking the peg out of the spring holder first. As soon as the least slip is perceptible, proceed thus:

4. Replace the cable nipple to the lever followed by re-adjustment of the midway cable adjuster to take up all play (but no more). Tighten the lock-nut; refit the adjuster tool to the spring holder and turn the wheel forward a little at a time until the cable is free by $\frac{1}{8}$–$\frac{3}{16}$ in. from the casing without operating the clutch mechanism. (*See also* earlier description of clutch adjustment, page 89.)

The Chain Cover. Do not overfill this. For actual racing leave out the chain case drain plug provided there is a separate continuous drip feed to the inner side of the chain just ahead of the clutch sprocket. Best method: fit a small auxiliary tank with a double outlet to the ends of the rollers. Control the flow with a needle valve or a 65–70 c.c. carburettor jet to give 6–8 drops per minute from each pipe.

Work on the Engine. This must all be directed at the reduction of friction losses. Start with the flywheel assembly; verify for freedom in the main bearings when the crankcase is hot. Correct the shimming if needed, remembering there is a pre-load of 0·004 in. with the crankcase cold. If a new big-end or parts such as rollers are fitted, check the bearings with a crankpin fitted into one flywheel so that the cage is accessible. With the con-rod assembly on the crankpin it should be possible to turn the con-rod round while holding the cage and rollers stationary. Slight up and down play will be perceptible in the bearings when dry. Check con-rod alignment; distortion is unlikely but the least misalignment will cause heavy drag and power loss.

Piston rings must bear evenly on the working faces and all round the lands. Factory replacements are correctly gapped. Rings can be lapped into the grooves with metal polish; be careful to clean it all away before final assembly. Do this cleaning with the rings in position as there is the risk of imparting a permanent set to them by removal or replacement. Prolonged racing with the Venom calls for the Clubman oil control ring number SL. 3/68.

The piston crown after running should show a dry appearance without traces of burnt oil. Severe loss of power results from oil either passing the rings or down the valve guides and so contaminating the fuel.

Internal Parts. Ample clearance between flywheels and crankcase is correct and nothing is gained by polishing internal parts. Engine flywheels previous to Viper VR. 1144 and Venom VM. 1114 were of larger diameter with less side clearance from the crankcase. Veloce Ltd. will modify and re-balance flywheels from such engines; no other modification or re-balance is permissible.

Inlet Exhaust Ports and Valves. Ports are ground at the factory to a smooth finish after the valve seats have been fitted; note that correct shape is more important than a high degree of surface finish. If the work is very carefully done the inlet can be narrowed and the inner edge blended with the port without reducing the seat base diameter. The width of the exhaust seat must not be reduced. In grinding valves get a smooth matt finish on the seats and do not attempt to polish them. Nimonic "80" exhaust valves are now standard equipment on Viper and Venom and can be obtained for earlier models.

Valve springs should be replaced if they have had considerable service. Fitting of new springs, or any new parts—valves or collars—or truing up or renewal of valve seats makes necessary checking the installed length of the springs. Measure between the top face of the valve spring bottom fixing collar, and the underside of the loop of the spring where it rests beneath the top collar: this distance must not exceed 0·562 in. and should lie between 0·542–0·562 in. Correct by fitting shims or washers between the bottom spring mounting and the cylinder head over the valve guides.

Reduction in spring poundage either through weakness or incorrect installation will mean that valve bounce sets in at much less than the possible maximum engine speed. This means considerable loss of power output as well as a risk of bent valves.

Compression Ratio. Compression plates are fitted during production, to suit ratios to premium fuels of 80/100 octane. Standard compression space volumes are: Viper, 47–48 c.c.; Viper Clubman, 42–43 c.c.; Venom, 68–69 c.c.; Venom Clubman 64–65 c.c. Compression plates are of 0·01 and 0·031 in. The Viper with 0·01 plate shows a difference in volume of 1·04 c.c., and with a 0·031 plate, of 3·24 c.c. On the Venom a 0·01 plate makes a difference of 1·48 c.c., and the 0·031 plate one of 4·6 c.c.

Slightly raising the compression ratio must be accompanied, if the bore is worn, by removal of the small ridge from the top edge. For prolonged racing the standard split-skirt piston can be replaced by the full-skirt Clubman type. This, having greater clearance, will reduce drag, but with some rise in mechanical noise.

Valve Timing. It is not possible to verify this accurately with both push-rods in place, nor with ordinary clearances. Therefore remove the inlet push-rod while checking the exhaust, and vice versa. Increase exhaust clearance to 0·052 in., and inlet to 0·053 in. and the following will result—

Inlet opens 45° B.T.D.C., closes 55° A.B.D.C. Exhaust opens 65° B.B.D.C., closes 35° A.T.D.C.

After checking, reset valves to running clearances (0·005 in. for both inlet and exhaust). Scrambler clearances are somewhat more: inlet 0·006 in., exhaust 0·008 in., settings which can also be used on other machines for prolonged speed work.

Check the contact-breaker gap before timing the ignition, and see that all backlash is taken out of the gears; correct setting is 38° before T.D.C. on full advance (the MSS model takes 36°).

Reducing Weight. Some owners carry out extensive work to lighten reciprocating parts; but it is not to be recommended unless the operator has had a great deal of experience. Removal of material at points where it causes changes in shape or section, may curtail the reliability of the component and even result in its failure under load.

Silencers. These are usually obligatory at Clubman-type events: a special silencer and exhaust pipe are available. The pipe is bent, and the silencer fixing modified, to increase ground clearance. They do not otherwise differ from standard parts, but cannot be fitted in conjunction with standard footrests and pedals.

The baffle or shroud tubes of the silencer should never be altered; the design has been carefully worked out to give the best power output consistent with reasonable silencing. Experience shows that any alteration always reduces the power and speed —never the contrary.

Open-exhaust races offer a choice between constant-diameter pipes and megaphones. The pipe is better for standing-start events, and sprints; the megaphone gives a better top-end power output at the expense of lower-end output. The length of pipe is important and measurements quoted in the appended tables of carburettor settings are down the centre of the pipe.

Changes in the exhaust system make resetting of the carburettor essential; settings as quoted must be considered as a guide only. Final setting must reckon with the course, altitude and weather conditions. Error should be on the slightly rich side, to avoid risk of overheating even at the expense of ultimate maximum speed. In races of any great length, heat builds up and may not become excessive until the major part of the distance has been covered.

The following are Veloce's sparking plug recommendations, in the KLG range. For hard sustained high speeds on the road with silencer—FE220. For racing on shorter circuits, the engine being frequently throttled back—FE 250. For Clubman racing, using full throttle for long periods—FE 280.

CARBURETTOR SETTINGS (see also page 108)

VENOM MODEL: NORMAL SETTINGS IN GREAT BRITAIN

Type of Exhaust System	1 3/16 in. 10TT9 carburettor		1 3/16 in./389/15 monobloc	
A Exhaust pipe and silencer (Clubman type 3 ft 5 in. down centre line)	Main jet Needle jet Needle position Throttle valve	370 109 3 4	Main jet Needle jet Needle position Throttle valve	330 1065 4 3½
B Megaphone exhaust: length of pipe and megaphone 4 ft 2 in. down centre line	Main jet Needle jet Needle position Throttle valve	390 109 3 5	Main jet Needle jet Needle position Throttle valve	370 1065 4 3½
C Open exhaust pipe length 4 ft 0 in. to 4 ft 4 in. down centre line	Main jet Needle jet Needle position Throttle valve	390 109 3 7	Main jet Needle jet Needle position Throttle valve	370 1065 4 4½

SUGGESTED ALTERNATIVE SETTINGS (VENOM ONLY)

Exhaust System—				
A	Main jet Needle jet Needle position Throttle valve 3, 4, or 5	330 to 370 109 3	Main jet Needle jet Needle position Throttle valve	330 to 370 1065 4 2½, 3½ or 4½
B	Main jet Needle jet Needle position Throttle valve 4, 5 or 6	370 to 410 109 3	Main jet Needle jet Needle position Throttle valve	350 to 390 1065 4 2½, 3½ or 4½
C	Main jet Needle jet Needle position Throttle valve 6, 7 or 8	370 to 410 109 3	Main jet Needle jet Needle position Throttle valve	350 to 390 1065 4 3½, 4½ or 5½

VIPER MODEL: NORMAL SETTINGS IN GREAT BRITAIN

Exhaust System—	1 1/16 in. TT9 carburettor		1 1/16 in. 371/61 monobloc	
A	Main jet Needle jet Needle position Throttle valve	340 109 3 4	Main jet Needle jet Needle position Throttle valve	270 1065 2 3½
B	Main jet Needle jet Needle position Throttle valve	360 109 4 7	Main jet 310 to 330 Needle jet 1065 Needle position 2 Throttle valve 3½ or 4½	
C	Main jet Needle jet Needle position Throttle valve	360 109 3 7	Main jet 310 to 330 Needle jet 1065 Needle position 3 Throttle valve 3½ or 4	

VENOM THRUXTON 500

DEVELOPED from the Venom Clubman Veeline during successful attempts on the 12- and 24-hour records, and from other racing events at home and abroad, the Venom Thruxton 500 is a machine which can be used on the road and then quickly stripped down for racing. Higher gear and compressions ratios, a $1\frac{3}{8}$ in. Amal G.P. carburettor and a re-designed inlet valve and cylinder-head area have produced 41 b.h.p. from the engine at 6,200 r.p.m. General specifications will be found on page 65. Since basically the machine is the Venom of 86 × 86 m.m., the Thruxton remains similar to this model in most respects.

Inlet Port Design. A new inlet valve of 2 in. outside diameter, in conjunction with a radiused Austenitic iron seat, has a modified angle so that even if the engine is accidentally over-revved the valves cannot touch. The combustion chamber has a flatter form and other features are an inlet port of steeper downdraught and greater swirl angle, special cam followers and lightened valve gear.

Special Cycle Features. These include double-leading-shoe brakes with coupled actuating cams, scoop cooling and drilled hub. The Velocette teleforks have two-way damping and rubber gaiters. Aluminium wheel-rims and narrow mudguards contribute to the weight saving which the Thruxton shows over the Venom Clubman—375 lb as against 404 lb. A Dolphin-type fairing is available for the 500.

FIG. 54. THE 500 C.C. VENOM THRUXTON

Index

OTHER MOTORCYCLE MANUALS AVAILABLE IN THIS SERIES

AJS (BOOK OF) ALL MODELS 1955-1965:
350cc & 500cc Singles ~ Models 16,16S,18, 18S

ARIEL WORKSHOP MANUAL 1933-1951:
All single, twin & 4 cylinder models

ARIEL (BOOK OF) MAINTENANCE & REPAIR MANUAL 1932-1939:
LF3, LF4, LG, NF3, NF4, NG, OG, VA, VA3, VA4, VB, VF3, VF4, VG,
Red Hunter LH, NH, OH, VH & Square Four 4F, 4G, 4H

BMW FACTORY WORKSHOP MANUAL R27, R28:
English, German, French and Spanish text

BMW FACTORY WORKSHOP MANUAL R50, R50S, R60, R69S:
Also includes a supplement for the USA models: R50US, R60US, R69US.
English, German, French and Spanish text

BSA PRE-WAR SINGLES & TWINS (BOOK OF) 1936-1939:
All Pre-War single & twin cylinder SV & OHV models through 1939
150cc, 250cc, 350cc, 500cc, 600cc, 750cc & 1,000cc

BSA SINGLES (BOOK OF) 1945-1954:
OHV & SV 250cc, 350cc, 500cc & 600cc, Groups B, C & M

BSA SINGLES (BOOK OF) 1955-1967:
B31, B32, B33, B34 and "Star" B40 & SS90

BSA 250cc SINGLES (BOOK OF) 1954-1970:
B31, B32, B33, B34 and "Star" B40 & SS90

BSA TWINS (BOOK OF) 1948-1962:
All 650cc & 500cc twins

DUCATI OHC FACTORY WORKSHOP MANUAL:
160 Junior Monza, 250 Monza, 250 GT, 250 Mark 3, 250 Mach 1, 250 SCR &
350 Sebring

HONDA 250 & 305cc FACTORY WORKSHOP MANUAL:
C.72 C.77 CS.72, CS.77, CB.72, CB.77 [HAWK]

HONDA 125 & 150cc FACTORY WORKSHOP MANUAL:
C.92, CS.92, CB.92, C.95 & CA.95

HONDA 90 (BOOK OF) ALL MODELS UP TO 1966:
All 90cc variations including the S90, CM90, C200, S65, Trail 90 & C65
models

HONDA 50cc FACTORY WORKSHOP MANUAL: C.100

HONDA 50cc FACTORY WORKSHOP MANUAL: C.110

HONDA (BOOK OF) MAINTENANCE & REPAIR 1960-1966:
50cc C.100, C.102, C.110 & C.114 ~ 125cc C.92 & CB.92
250cc C.72 & CB.72 ~ 305cc CB.77

LAMBRETTA (BOOK OF) MAINTENANCE & REPAIR:
125 & 150cc, all models up to 1958, except model "48".

**NORTON FACTORY TWIN CYLINDER WORKSHOP MANUAL
1957-1970:** *Lightweight Twins:* 250cc Jubilee, 350cc Navigator and 400cc
Electra and the *Heavyweight Twins:* Model 77, 88, 88SS, 99, 99SS, Sports
Special, Manxman, Mercury, Atlas, G15, P11, N15, Ranger (P11A).

NORTON (BOOK OF) MAINTENANCE & REPAIR 1932-1939:
All Pre-War SV, OHV and OHC models: 16H, 16I, 18, 19, 20, 50, 55, ES2,
CJ, CSI, International 30 & 40

SUZUKI 200 & 250cc FACTORY WORKSHOP MANUAL:
250cc T20 [X-6 Hustler] ~ 200cc T200 [X-5 Invader & Sting Ray Scrambler]

SUZUKI 250cc FACTORY WORKSHOP MANUAL: 250cc ~ T10

TRIUMPH (BOOK OF) MAINTENANCE & REPAIR 1935-1939:
All Pre-War single & twin cylinder models: L2/1, 2/1, 2/5, 3/1, 3/2, 3/5, 5/1,
5/2, 5/3, 5/4, 5/5, 5/10, 6/1, Tiger 70, 80, 90 & 2H. Tiger 70C, 3S & 3H,
Tiger 80C & 5H, Tiger 90C, 6S, 2HC & 3SC, 5T & 5S and T100

TRIUMPH 1937-1951 WORKSHOP MANUAL (A. St. J. Masters):
Covers rigid frame and sprung hub single cylinder SV & OHV and twin
cylinder OHV pre-war, military, and post-war models

TRIUMPH 1945-1955 FACTORY WORKSHOP MANUAL NO.11:
Covers pre-unit, twin-cylinder rigid frame, sprung hub, swing-arm and 350cc,
500cc & 650cc.

VELOCETTE (BOOK OF) MAINTENANCE & REPAIR:
Covers LE Mk. I, II, & III, Valiant, Vogue, MOV, MAC, KSS, KTS, Viper,
Venom & Thruxton. Includes some limited material on the Viceory scooter

VESPA (BOOK OF) MAINTENANCE & REPAIR 1946-1959:
All 125cc & 150cc models including 42/L2 & Gran Sport

VINCENT WORKSHOP MANUAL 1935-1955:
All Series A, B & C Models

www.VelocePress.com

Lightning Source UK Ltd.
Milton Keynes UK
UKHW010323280219
337958UK00004B/22/P